D0901039

*Reading Medieval Latin with the
Legend of Barlaam and Josaphat*

Reading Medieval Latin with the Legend of Barlaam and Josaphat

Donka D. Markus

University of Michigan Press
Ann Arbor

Copyright © 2018 by Donka D. Markus
All rights reserved

This book may not be reproduced, in whole or in part, including illustrations, in any form
(beyond that copying permitted by Sections 107 and 108 of the U.S. Copyright Law and except by
reviewers for the public press), without written permission from the publisher.

Published in the United States of America by the
University of Michigan Press
Manufactured in the United States of America
Printed on acid-free paper
First published July 2018

A CIP catalog record for this book is available from the British Library.

Library of Congress Cataloging-in-Publication Data

Names: Jacobus, de Voragine, approximately 1229–1298, author. | Markus, Donka D., editor,
    writer of added commentary.
Title: Reading medieval Latin with the legend of Barlaam and Josaphat / [edited and supplied
    with commentary by] Donka D. Markus.
Other titles: Michigan classical commentaries.
Description: Ann Arbor : University of Michigan Press, 2018. | Series: Michigan classical
    commentaries | In Latin, with introduction and commentary in English.
Identifiers: LCCN 2017059438| ISBN 9780472073849 (hardcover : alk. paper) |
    ISBN 9780472053841 (pbk. : alk. paper)
Subjects: LCSH: Latin language—Readers. | Barlaam, Saint (Legendary character)—Legends—
    Early works to 1800. | Josaphat, Saint (Legendary character)—Legends—Early works to
    1800. | Christian saints—India—Legends—Early works to 1800. | Martyrs—India—
    Legends—Early works to 1800. | LCGFT: Legends.
Classification: LCC PA2095 .J33   2018 | DDC 477—dc23
LC record available at https://lccn.loc.gov/2017059438

In memoriam matris Marta Bur
végtelen hálával mivel mindnyájunk útjai a Végtelenbe vezetnek
(infinitas tibi gratias ago quoniam omnium semitae nostrum directae
ad Infinitatem sunt).

Acknowledgments

The idea for this reader started at a public lecture given by D. Lopez and P. McCracken in the winter of 2015, where they introduced their new book, *In Search of the Christian Buddha: How an Asian Sage Became a Medieval Saint* (New York: W. W. Norton, 2014). I was fascinated with the topic, and since I was teaching a fourth semester Late Latin class I assigned portions of Jacobus de Voragine's version of the legend to the students in the class as final projects. These student projects from winter 2015 became the foundation of this reader. I am grateful to the students, both graduate and undergraduate, in my classes of winter 2016 and winter 2017 who inspired me to continue work on the reader and to prepare it for publication. Megan Behrend and Ryan Kelly contributed valuably to fine-tuning the commentary.

I thank P. McCracken for the encouragement to pursue this project. I am also grateful to the staff of the University of Michigan Press for recognizing the value of the reader when it was in its early stages, and especially to Ellen Bauerle for her help and guidance through the process of publication.

I thank my colleague Deborah P. Ross for being such a supportive and understanding colleague over the years. I am also grateful to Sara Ahbel-Rappe, Catherine Brown, Ellen Poteet, and Dione Greenberg for their valuable feedback and intellectually stimulating engagement with my work.

I also owe gratitude to the audience of the Latin Pedagogy panel at the 2016 Classical Association of the Middle West and South, which received with interest my paper on "Educating Global Citizens through the Latin Translation of the Life of Barlaam and Josaphat" and encouraged me to pursue the publication of this text. My conversation with John Gruber-Miller at the conference was the most decisive factor in solidifying my resolve to take this project outside the walls of my own classroom.

I thank SISMEL—Edizioni del Galluzzo in Florence for granting me the permission to print the Latin text from P. Maggioni's 2007 Latin edition of Jacobus de Voragine's *Legenda Aurea*.

I am also immensely grateful to the reviewers of the first draft of this project. Without their valuable suggestions for improvements, the quality of the final product would have suffered. The problems that still remain are my own responsibility.

Cecily Hilsdale (McGill University) helped me identify suitable images for inclusion in the book. I am grateful to Carrie Wood and Jacqueline Stimson for carefully proofreading the manuscript during its final stages.

I am most grateful for the moral and financial support given to me by the Department of Classical Studies at the University of Michigan, especially to its chair, Sara Forsdyke, who found the necessary funding when it was most needed.

It is to my mentor, Charles Witke, that I am most indebted.

Contents

Preface

This intermediate Latin reader is designed to strengthen students' reading skills through an accessible and entertaining text. The content of the legend of Barlaam and Josaphat is conducive to developing students' narrative imagination and their awareness of textual transmission and cross-cultural translation. Thus, this reader addresses the Communication, the Cultures, the Connections, the Comparisons, and the Communities goal of the World-Readiness Standards for Learning Languages.[1]

The reader is intended for students who have taken a full year of elementary Latin, or an intensive course covering the basics of Latin grammar, and who have acquired some experience in reading Classical Latin prose through an author like Caesar. However, the extensive vocabulary and commentary make it possible to enjoy the legend of Barlaam and Josaphat immediately after the successful completion of an elementary Latin course.

The vocabulary and commentary also make this reader suitable for independent study and home-school settings. Motivated learners can look up unfamiliar terms in the two grammars that the commentary refers to throughout and can consult the explanations of Late Latin features at the end of the book.

The text included in this reader is Jacobus de Voragine's abridged Latin version of the legend of Saints Barlaam and Josaphat. The Latin of Jacobus, a 13th-century compiler, offers excellent opportunities for the systematic learning of the peculiarities of Late and Medieval Latin. Typically, one has to read many texts and take a survey course to encounter the elements of Late Latin that distinguish it from Classical Latin. This text, however, conveniently contains most of these elements and is thus a suitable introduction to the subject.[2]

---

1. Available from the American Council for the Teaching of Foreign Languages (ACTFL) website. The application of the World Readiness Standards for Learning Languages to the Classical Languages is called *Standards for Classical Language Learning*, available from the American Classical League.

2. The problem of how best to teach Medieval Latin in a systematic way was discussed in the

The high quality of Jacobus's Latin makes it appropriate for training readers of Classical Latin as well, for it contains most features found in the best Classical authors. Thus, the legend can offer valuable experience with the language before students proceed to more complex texts. With its occasional periodic sentences, rich stylistic devices, and authentic Classical word order, it can serve as superb preparation and training for the reading and deeper appreciation of Cicero and complex rhetorical prose in general. Since the story is engaging and requires minimal introduction, readers can focus on learning the intricacies of the language, most of them common to both Classical and Late/Medieval Latin.[3]

Both high school and college teachers who want to illustrate the global significance of Latin can incorporate into their curricula the legend of Barlaam and Josaphat, which is now gaining broader readership and appreciation due to the recent scholarship about its adventurous history.[4] Since many of the fables included in the legend are the common heritage of many cultures and religions, I hope that the very nature of this textbook and the content of its readings will make Latin an attractive subject to students of more diverse backgrounds and will highlight the important role of Latin in the development of humanity's global self-consciousness.

The legend unifies a collection of colorful fables that demonstrate the vigorous East-West contacts in the premodern period. It probes the deepest questions about the meaning of human life lived with full awareness of its transitory nature. It juxtaposes the two extreme responses to this transience, namely the life of self-mortification and the life of self-gratification. While it endorses the life of renunciation and asceticism, it also gives voice to many commonly shared ethical principles and philosophical truths, vividly conveyed through its parables, fables, and anecdotes. Some of these are: the lasting value of charity, compassion, and kindness to all, especially to those of lower social status; the joys of gratitude, honesty, friendship; the value of critical thinking for detecting falsehoods, fake stories, and deceptive appearances; the wisdom to discern that not all that glitters is gold; the insight that what is impermanent and unreal creates a desire for what is permanent and real.

Explicitly associated with India, the legend of Barlaam and Josaphat enjoyed tremendous popularity and passed through translations into Persian, Arabic, Georgian, Greek, Latin, and, from Latin, into all western European languages. From Arabic, an adapted Hebrew version was made.[5] From Greek,

---

1970s and 1980s. For the problem itself, see Lanham (1975). Later, in response to Clark (1979), Lanham (1980) addressed the need for a single text that illustrates most features of Postclassical Latin.

3. The problems with the terms "Late Latin" (discussed by Adams (2011) 257–58) and with "Medieval Latin" (discussed by Dinkova-Brunn (2011) 284–85) are known to me, but I chose them as practical placeholders for the purposes of this reader.

4. Lopez and McCracken (2014).

5. Smith (1981) 10.

it was translated into Church Slavonic, Armenian, and Christian Arabic. There are sixty versions of the legend in the major languages of Europe, the Christian East, and Africa.[6]

The legend took on new emphases and meanings as cultural, geographical, and political contexts shifted. It illustrates how each generation and culture enriches the received traditions from the past. It does not teach a religious truth specific to any one religious tradition. Instead, it demonstrates the irresistible power of storytelling itself and shows how stories addressing existential human concerns and aspirations circulate among different cultures and religions.[7]

Of the eleven Latin versions of the legend of Saints Barlaam and Josaphat, I chose the 13th-century version in Jacobus de Voragine's hagiographical collection, *The Golden Legend* (*Legenda Aurea*) because of its brevity and the accessible quality of its Latin. Intermediate Latin students can read this 5,000-word long text in about eight to ten weeks.

Ways to Use This Intermediate Reader

I envision the following ways of using this text:

1. High school or college students who wish to acquire extensive reading experience with an intermediate level original Latin text will read through the narrative sequentially in eight to ten weeks. The text contains an abundance of grammatical features and rhetorical devices commonly found in Classical authors, but the engaging storyline will contribute to a faster reading pace and will provide opportunities for developing students' narrative imagination.

2. Students taking intermediate courses with multiple authors can read selections from this text either as prepared or as sight-reading practice. The redundancies in the grammatical commentary and vocabulary are designed to accommodate these users.

3. Students who want to learn how to read Medieval Latin manuscripts will focus on the version of the text with the original orthography printed in front. By starting with this text, they will practice detecting words spelled differently from their equivalents in Classical Latin. After identifying the words with Medieval Latin orthography, they can compare their findings with the commentary version of the text where all words are spelled according to Classical Latin norms. Thus, the normalized version will serve as a key. With consistent practice, such students can gradually gain valuable experience reading Medieval Latin as it appears in the manuscripts.

---

6. Almond (1987) 391.

7. Cf. Lopez and McCracken (2014) 13.

Abbreviations and Formatting Conventions Used in the Commentary

Abbreviations used in the commentary:

A&G = *Allen and Greenough's New Latin Grammar for Schools and Colleges* (2003 [1903]), ed. J. B. Greenough, G. L. Kittredge, A. A. Howard, and Benjamin L. D'Ooge. Updated for Focus by Anne Mahoney. Newburyport, MA: Focus Publishing. **Numbers refer to chapter, not page**.

CL = Classical Latin

DO = direct object

G. = Grammar section. All Late Latin features are explained and illustrated in the Grammar section printed at the back of the reader. The Commentary refers to this Grammar throughout (e.g., G. 2.2).

Introd. = Introduction printed at the beginning of the reader.

LL = Late Latin/Medieval Latin

Formatting conventions used in the commentary:

1. The spelling of the underlined words is adjusted to reflect Classical Latin norms. The original spelling can be found in the version of the text printed at the beginning of the reader.

2. The **bolded terms** can be found in S. C. Shelmerdine's *Introduction to Latin*. I assume that students are familiar with the bolded grammatical terminology (e.g., **indirect command, relative noun clause**, etc.). For the more obscure grammatical categories that are **not** included in S. C. Shelmerdine, I reference Allen and Greenough's *Latin Grammar* (A&G). The terms taken from Allen and Greenough are not bolded.

Detailed Table of Contents
to the Introduction

Introduction

1. The Cross-Cultural Nature of the Legend

1.1. THE JOURNEY OF BARLAAM AND JOSAPHAT THROUGH TIME AND PLACE

The legend of Prince Josaphat and his teacher Barlaam has a distinct appeal and relevance today. It is a paradigmatic tale about a young person's quest for truth through a convoluted labyrinth of lies, deceptive narratives, and fake characters. Josaphat's father, a powerful king, fearing that his son will become a Christian ascetic, raises Josaphat in the artificial and treacherous environment of an isolated pleasure palace. To prevent his son from embarking on a quest for answers to life's excruciating questions about illness, suffering, old age, and death, the king educates him within the fragile bubble of a fake narrative that attempts to erase life's most painful and shocking facts from his lived experience. Predictably, the false construct collapses at the young man's first field trip outside the palace. It is at this point that a sage appears and starts to instruct the prince in his search for answers. The lessons of the sage, expressed in parables, end with the conversion of the prince and his renunciation of an earthly kingdom in favor of a heavenly one.

The legend's link to the life-story of the Buddha became widely known only in the middle of the 19th century,[1] but research shows that most of its signature elements are absent from the oldest version of Buddha's life and are, therefore, later additions.[2] Both the life of the Buddha and the legend of Barlaam and Josaphat share motifs that belong to the universal bank of wisdom-tales transmitted from culture to culture and from religion to religion through storytelling over time. As Lopez and McCracken aptly comment, "religions circulate among stories."[3] We are dealing "with a work in which the ideals

---

1. Isolated individuals had knowledge of this as early as the 15th century. Cf. the commentary to chapter 1.
2. Cf. Lopez and McCracken (2014) 221.
3. Lopez and McCracken (2014) 13.

of renunciation and the ascetic way of life are woven around certain salient features of the traditional life of the Buddha-elect, a whole series of extraneous fables and parables being inserted from other Indian and oriental sources in the course of the work's transmission."[4]

This appealing story was an object of creative retelling even before it made its way to the West, and when it arrived to the Middle East and Europe, the momentum of its movement did not slow down, but continues to our day. From two Arabic, then two Georgian and finally a Greek version, it was translated into Latin, which paved the way to its remarkable influence in Europe.

The Middle High German poet Rudolf von Elms wrote a romance in verse called *Barlaam and Josaphat* (ca. 1220).[5] It is around the same time that Gui de Cambrai produced his Old French version of *Barlaam and Josaphat* in verse,[6] one of two other Old French renditions in verse and seven more in prose.[7] Also in the early 13th century, Abraham ibn Hasdāy in Barcelona produced a Hebrew version of the legend, called *The Book of the Prince and the Hermit*. It became widespread in the Jewish world with two editions appearing in the 16th century, which were translated into German and Polish in the 18th century. The legend reemerged again in a Yiddish rendition in the 19th century.[8] In Spain, the 16th–17th-century dramatist Lope de Vega turned the legend into a dramatic play.[9]

Many of the individual fables included in the legend acquired a life of their own and became part of sermons, historical and moral compilations, and collections of stories throughout the pre-modern period.[10] A variation on the fable about the four chests appears in Boccacio's *Decameron* (Day 10, first tale).[11] William Shakespeare turned the four chests into three caskets in his *Merchant of Venice* (act 2, scene 9), probably using William Caxton's 15th-century rendition of Barlaam and Josaphat into English.[12]

In the 20th century, the Harvard theologian W. C. Smith called *Barlaam and Josaphat* an example of "world theology," "noting that the story, making its way from Buddhists to Manicheans to Muslims to Christians, had inspired Tolstoy, who wrote about it in his *Confession*."[13] The famous Russian aristocrat and writer Leo Tolstoy (1828–1910) experienced a drastic spiritual conversion

---

4. Lang (1958) 12–13, cited in Almond (1987) 397.
5. Schulz (1981) 136–37.
6. Now available in a contemporary English translation by McCracken (2014).
7. McCracken (2014) xv.
8. Smith (1981) 10. Cf. Lopez and McCracken (2014) 170–71.
9. Lopez and McCracken (2014) 11.
10. Almond (1987) 292.
11. Bolton (1958) 359 fn. 2.
12. Almond (1987) 291.
13. Lopez and McCracken (2014) 207.

after reading the legend of Baralaam and Josaphat. He was most impressed by the allegory of the man in the well. Just like Josaphat in the legend, he "turned from worldly success to the ascetic life of non-violence, poverty and social service."[14] Tolstoy's work, in turn, greatly influenced the young Mohandas Gandhi (1869–1948), leader of the Indian independence movement against British rule, and inspiration behind many nonviolent civil disobedience movements across the world.[15] Thus, the legend, which started out in the East, kept circulating between East and West. Gandhi's contemporary, the German writer Herman Hesse (1877–1962), based his literary masterpiece *Siddhartha* (1922) on this legend.

1.2. VERSIONS OF THE LEGEND

The origin of the legend of Barlaam and Josaphat has been the object of painstaking research by generations of scholars since the middle of the 19th century, and here I offer just a brief glimpse into the findings of this research to date.

The journey of the legend through time and place involved linguistic changes to the name of its main protagonist. He starts out as the *bodhisattva* in Sanskrit. *Bodhisattva*, which in Sankrit means "one who aspires to enlightenment," is the main epithet of Prince Siddhārtha, the future Buddha ("one who is awake"). *Bodhisattva* appears as Bodisaf in the Manichean versions[16] and as Būdhāsaf in the Arabic ones where al-Budd is a prophet whose teachings and life Būdhāsaf wants to emulate. Būdhāsaf becomes Iodasaph in the Georgian version, which erases al-Budd. Then Iodasaph becomes Ioasaph in Greek and Iosaphat in Latin.[17] In English, we spell the name of the protagonist as "Josaphat."

1.2.1. The Indian Buddhist Version about Prince Siddhārtha (*bodhisattva*, known later as the Buddha)[18]

The Buddha lived and taught in northern India in the 5th century BCE. There are many versions of his life. However, none of these versions can be conclusively identified as the original Buddhist source of the Barlaam and Josaphat legend.[19]

---

14. Smith (1981) 6.

15. Lopez and McCracken (2014) 207, cf. Smith (1981) 10–11.

16. Smith (1981) 9. Manichaeism was a gnostic dualistic sect that had its own prophet Mani (216–247 CE). It was one of the large world religions between the 3rd and the 7th centuries CE and spread from the Roman Empire in the West as far as China in the East.

17. Cf. Lopez and McCracken (2014) 54ff, 90ff, 122ff.

18. Cf. Lopez and McCracken (2014) 14–53.

19. Lopez (2014) xii, introduction to McCracken's translation of Gui de Cambrai's *Barlaam and Josaphat*.

For those wishing to compare Jacobus de Voragine's Christianized version with the best-known Buddhist versions of the life of the Buddha, I outline below those episodes of Buddha's life that differ from the plot of the legend included in this reader:[20]

- The future Buddha's father is not an ideological enemy. He does not persecute anyone and is not an ardent defender of idolatry. Instead, he just wants to ensure successful succession to his throne.
- Prince Siddhārtha grows up surrounded by all kinds of pleasures, including the company of attractive women, but after his discovery of disease, old age, and death, he in unable to enjoy these temporary pleasures. His response to them is that of detached piety rather than conflicted desire. In the later versions, the protagonists struggle against temptation while Siddhārtha's advanced spiritual state makes him impassive toward all enticements due to his realization of the decay and death beneath every beautiful appearance.
- Prince Siddhārtha is not celibate but has a wife. To show his virility, he begets a son before he renounces his luxurious life in search of enlightenment at age twenty-nine.
- He practices severe forms of asceticism and self-mortification for six years in the company of five other ascetics and nearly starves himself to death without attaining his goal. He realizes that he could die without attaining enlightenment, so he begs for alms in the nearby village and regains his strength and health. His companions leave him, thinking that he has given up.
- The Boddhisatva continues his search for enlightenment and attains it at age thirty-five under the sacred Bodhi tree, following his victory over Lust, Craving, and Discontent, the three daughters of Māra, the deity of desire and death.
- The enlightened Buddha preaches the middle way between harsh self-mortification and excessive self-gratification. He founds a monastic order and "although Buddhist monasticism might be seen, at least in its textual renditions, as a form of asceticism,"[21] the middle way between extremes remains central to the Buddhist tradition. The later versions of the legend emphasize ascetic piety without reference to the middle way.
- Prince Siddhārtha does not have a teacher similar to Barlaam, who is mentoring Josaphat. He receives instruction from two meditation teachers but quickly surpasses their attainments.

---

20. For more details, consult Lopez and McCracken (2014) 15–53.
21. Cf. Lopez and McCracken (2014) 222.

1.2.2. The Arabic Version of the Bilawhar and Būdhāsaf Legend

Buddhism spread not just to the North but also to the West, to Persia where the Indian legend travelled along the Silk Road. The Manicheans between the 3rd and 7th centuries were familiar with the tale, for "fragments of the story have been found in early collections of Manichean manuscripts." [22] At some point the legend was translated from the original Sanskrit or another Indian language into Middle Persian (Pahlavi). The now lost Persian translation was rendered into two Arabic versions sometime between 750 and 900.[23]

As it travelled from India to the Middle East, the legend underwent adaptations to accord with monotheistic beliefs.[24] Incremental changes, listed below, started creeping in and set the Arabic version of the legend apart from its earlier iterations:

- Both father and son are devoted to the prophet al-Budd and both believe that they are his true followers. They differ in their interpretation of al-Budd's teachings. The king believes that the prophet taught charity and goodness but did not require renunciation of the world.[25] By contrast, his son endorses "the people of the Religion" who profess an ascetic renunciation of worldly values.
- The father persecutes the ascetics, the followers of "the Religion." His son supports them.
- The figure of the teacher appears. The teacher is a monotheist. Much of the story consists of didactic exchanges between prince and teacher and then prince and father.
- The teacher exalts martyrdom and promotes ascetic values. He emphasizes the conflict of loyalty to an earthly king and to a spiritual lord. He also preaches adherence to a spiritual lineage that can be attained only through the rejection of the body.
- There is an episode of Būdhāsaf attaining enlightenment under a huge tree, but the description of that enlightenment is brief and vague.[26]
- Virginity and chastity are not as central to this version as to the Christian ones, but the prince fends off lust here as well. Būdhāsaf eventually begets a son who is to succeed his father on the throne while he can renounce the world.

---

22. Cf. Lopez and McCracken (2014) 222.
23. Cf. Lopez (2014) xi, introduction to McCracken's translation of Gui de Cambrai's *Barlaam and Josaphat*.
24. For more detail, cf. Lopez and McCracken (2014) 54–89.
25. Lopez and McCracken (2014) 75.
26. MacQueen (2001) 156.

1.2.3. The Georgian Version, the *Balavariani* about Balavhar and Iodasaph

After the Muslim conquest of Georgia (Iberia) in the 7th century, a period of turmoil and resistance to the conquerors followed. To escape the fighting, some Georgians travelled to Palestine and established monasteries there. Georgian monks from the monastery of St. Sabas in Jerusalem translated the legend from Arabic into Georgian in the 9th–10th century. An abridged version was created in the 11th century. Saints Balavhar and Iodasaph became part of the Georgian orthodox calendar as early as the 10th century.[27] The feast day of the two saints is May 19.

This is the first Christianized version of the legend and the new elements are as follows:

- Balavhar and Iodasaph become Christian saints.
- The prophet al-Budd is erased from this version.
- The enlightenment scene is also erased from this version.[28]
- The father (King Abenes) is an idol worshipper and a fierce persecutor of Christians. He is also extremely self-indulgent and given to pleasures. The conflict between the idolatrous king and his Christian son becomes very intense.
- The story is politicized as a revenge fantasy against the Arabic occupiers of Georgia who persecuted Christians.

1.2.4. The Greek Version of the Barlaam and Ioasaph Legend

The translation from Georgian into Greek is the work of an 11th-century anonymous Greek monk, possibly the Georgian St. Euthymius (d. 1028) from Mount Athos.[29] The beginning of the Greek version of the legend erroneously cites John the monk from the monastery of St. Sabas as its author. This John was identified with John of Damascus (Iohannes Damascenus) because many themes from the writings of the 8th-century saint and theologian can be found in the theological digressions of the Greek version of the legend. No one in the 11th century suspected that the legend had its origin in India. People believed in the authorship of John of Damascus until the 19th century because it gave authority and credibility to the legend.

John of Damascus died in 749, long before the Greek translation was made,[30] and therefore he could not have been the translator or the author. Whoever he

27. Almond (1987) 394.
28. MacQueen (2001) 156.
29. Cf. Lopez and McCracken (2014) 131.
30. Lopez and McCracken (2014) 127–30.

was, the monk who translated and adapted the legend to Greek acknowledges the significant role of oral transmission. He admits that he heard the legend from others: "Here ends this history, which I have written, to the best of my ability, even as I heard it from the truthful lips of worthy men who delivered it onto me."[31]

The storyline of the Greek version, as we now know, came from a Georgian original. The anonymous Georgian monks had already Christianized the Arabic tale. "The contribution of the Greek monk was to theologize it."[32] The Greek version weaves many theological treatises into Barlaam's instruction of Josaphat, into the debates between father and son (Abenner and Ioasaph), and into the debates between fake Barlaam (Nachor) and the king's orators (rhetors). The similarity of these theological elements with the writings of John of Damascus suggests that the translator from the Georgian version into Greek was familiar with the writings of the 8th-century saint.[33]

The monk who created the Greek version of the legend was also a masterful interpolator. He transmitted the *Apology of Aristides*, believed lost for centuries, to the readers of this legend. He inserted the *Apology* (i.e., "defense" from Greek *apologia*) into the speeches of fake Barlaam, the pagan magus Nachor who masterfully defends Christianity despite his original hostility to it (cf. commentary to chapters 213–219). The *Apology of Aristides*, mentioned in the 4th century by Eusebius of Caesarea and by Jerome, was believed lost for 1,500 years until it was rediscovered at the end of the 19th century and identified with Nachor's defense of the Christian faith in Barlaam and Ioasaph.[34] Thus, it turned out that thanks to the Greek interpolator, the *Apology of Aristides* had never been truly lost. The philosopher Aristides, a convert to Christianity, had delivered the *Apology* in defense of his faith before the Emperor Hadrian in Athens in 125 CE. The emperor was so impressed that he issued an order stopping the persecution of Christians without proper investigation and trial.[35] The *Apologia*, spanning eight pages in the Greek version and its Latin translations, is compressed to six sentences in Jacobus de Voragine's abridged version (chapters 213–219).

With such a long oral tradition behind them and theological teachings to support them, Barlaam and Josaphat could claim a legitimate place in the church calendar. The two saints are worshiped by the Russian Orthodox Church on November 19 and by the Greek Orthodox Church on August 26. While they

---

31. Woodward and Mattingly (1997) 609.
32. Lopez and McCracken (2014) 133.
33. Almond (1987) 401.
34. For the adventurous discovery of the *Apology of Aristides*, cf. Lopez and McCracken (2014) 134–36.
35. Lopez and McCracken (2014) 134.

were not officially canonized as saints in the Roman Catholic Church, they had a feast day that was celebrated on November 27 since at least the 16th century.[36] The legend enjoyed tremendous popularity between the 12th and the 16th centuries and the large number of its Latin versions attest to that.

1.2.5. The Latin Versions of the Barlaam and Iosaphat Legend

There are eleven Latin versions of the legend ranging from the 12th to the 16th century.[37] I listed here only the versions that preceded Jacobus de Voragine's 13th-century summary of the legend included in this reader. The first two versions are more or less faithful translations of the original Greek with minimal modifications to the content:

1. The monks in Amalfi (Italy) who were in close contact with Byzantium translated the Greek version into Latin as early as 1047 or 1048.[38] This translation was not circulated widely and only one manuscript of it survives today in Naples (the Neapolitan version), which cites Euphemius as its translator.[39]
2. A second anonymous Latin translation from the Greek, called *Vulgata*, made a century later (12th century) became widely read and formed the basis for all subsequent Latin versions, including the one of Jacobus de Voragine.[40]
3. Vincent de Beauvais (1190–1264), Jacobus de Voragine's older contemporary, wrote *Speculum Maius*, the main encyclopedia used in the Middle Ages. In the section on history (*Speculum Historiale*), he devoted more than half of entry XV to the life of Barlaam and Josaphat (chapters 1–64), followed by the sayings of the Desert Fathers of the 4th century CE (chapters 65–100).[41] His encyclopedic entry is about six times shorter than the anonymous Latin translation of the 12th century.
4. Jacobus de Voragine (1230–98) abridged the legend even further in comparison to the encyclopedic entry of Vincent de Beauvais. Because his

---

36. Almond (1987) 394.
37. They are listed in Sonet's edition (1949) 73, cf. de la Cruz Palma (2001) 31.
38. Cf. Lopez and McCracken (2014) 137.
39. Sonet (1949) 73.
40. There was one more translation of the legend from the original Greek into Latin by the 16th-century French theologian Jacque de Billy (cf. Sonet (1949) 97).
41. Beauvais's *Speculum maius* does not have a modern reprinting. Chapter 15 in the fourth volume of Vincent de Beauvais (1964), a facsimile reprint of a 17th-century *incunabulum*, contains the Barlaam and Josaphat legend. Vincent de Beauvais's Latin version of Barlaam and Josaphat can also be accessed online in a 1494 Venetian edition (Vincentius Bellovacensis, *Speculum historiale*. Venetiis: Hermannus Liechtenstein).

version is about thirty times shorter than the unabridged Latin versions and five to six times shorter than the version of Vincent de Beauvais, some of the transitions from one episode to another are awkward. Inconsistencies creep in. For example, in chapter 274, there is a mention of the sign of the cross that Josaphat made, but the episode where he made it is omitted; in chapter 279, we hear the name of Barachias for the first time, although it is assumed that the reader knows who he is. The missing elements can be recovered from the complete versions. This commentary provides help with the awkward transitions and omissions, which are very few.

2. Author and Work

2.1. JACOBUS DE VORAGINE (1230–98)

Jacobus de Voragine, also known as Giacomo da Varazze, was born in Italy in the town of Varazze near Genoa. At the age of fourteen (in 1244), he entered the Dominican Order of Preachers charged with fighting heresies. Jacobus rose through the ranks to become archbishop of Genoa (1292). He acquired a reputation for holiness[42] and was known as "peacemaker and father to the poor."[43] He was beatified in 1816 and is venerated as a saint in Genoa.

He wrote *Chronicle on the History of Genoa* (*Chronicon januense*) and many sermons, but he is best known for his *Golden Legend* (*Legenda Aurea*), which he completed before reaching the age of forty.[44]

2.2. THE *GOLDEN LEGEND* (*LEGENDA AUREA*) COLLECTION

The *Golden Legend* (*Legenda Aurea*), originally called *Legenda Sanctorum* or *Readings on the Saints*,[45] is a hagiographical collection consisting of 181 lives of saints (hagiographies) arranged according to the religious calendar. The *legenda* in the title (gerundive from Latin *lego*) is intended to convey that these lives were essential, required readings. The legend of Barlaam and Josaphat is toward the end of the collection (item 180), but its length gives it an unusual prominence. Only four lives are longer than the life of Saints Barlaam and Josaphat. These are the lives of Saint Paul, Saint Gregory the Great, Saint Augustine, and Saint Dominic, the founder of Jacobus's religious order.[46]

Jacobus was not a creative thinker. His originality lay in his gift for

---

42. Reames (1985) 15.
43. Ryan (1993) xiii.
44. Reames (1985) 193.
45. Ryan (1993) xiii.
46. MacQueen (2001) 159.

compilation from some 130 sources, dated between the 2nd and the 13th century.[47] His reluctance to innovate and change the received tradition is of the greatest value to us because he faithfully reproduces earlier stories which otherwise would have been lost.[48] The contemporary English translator of the *Legenda* summarizes the main emphasis of the work as follows:

> His overall subject was the dealings of God with humankind—with salvation history as it revealed itself in God's agents and instruments, the saints.[49]

The *Golden Legend* is a history of God's saving power working through those most receptive to him. But it also became a popular reading and a source of religious inspiration. Between the 13th and early 16th century, it was the equivalent of a medieval best-seller, with over one thousand manuscripts of it surviving today.[50] It also had 156 printed editions between 1470 and 1500 alone.[51] The fact that "the cult of the saints reached a major turning point around the year 1270"[52] was a contributing factor to the work's popularity.

The *Golden Legend* suggests that in salvation history fiction can be more persuasive than fact. This very much applies to Barlaam and Josaphat, who had never lived outside the pages of their entertaining story. Still, their legend was one of the best-known lives of saints in the Latin West. A prominent theme in the legend is the conflict between secular and religious authority. Josaphat has to negotiate his relationship to his powerful father, King Avenir, on the one hand, and his teacher Barlaam wielding spiritual power over him, on the other. For the medieval reader, the conflict between king and papacy was a historical reality.

If evaluated with the scientific standards of historical accuracy and faithfulness to its sources, Jacobus's *Golden Legend* will be found sorely lacking. A number of church historians and theologians in the 17th century already realized that it was a spiritual fiction, a story, not history.[53] Jacobus drew a lot of criticism from all sides, but his defenders and admirers argue that he ought to be evaluated "as educator of the laity rather than as a historian."[54] After all, the genre of the work is legend, "compounded in large part of the repetition, from one generation to the next, of supposed truths which no one has quite bothered

---

47. Ryan (1993) xiv.
48. Ryan (1993) xv.
49. Ryan (1993) xiv.
50. MacQueen (2001) 159e.
51. Reames (1985) 4. Cf. MacQueen (2001) 159.
52. Reames (1985) 198.
53. Almond (1987) 395.
54. Reames (1985) 25.

to verify."[55] Still, these unverified supposed truths inspired and sustained the hope and faith of generations of storytellers, readers, and audiences. Calling the *Legenda* "almost a cultural institution"[56] captures well its pervasive influence. It was translated and adapted to a number of European languages: Old French, Spanish, Italian, Provencal, English, Dutch, High and Low German, Bohemian, and so on. It became an integral part of the dramatic and visual arts and today is a valuable source for students of "medieval mystery plays and miracle plays" and "for the study of medieval statuary and stained glass."[57]

In light of Jacobus's role as transmitter of ancient cultural treasures and lore and in light of the tremendous influence of his work, the modern reader has to overlook the limitations in his intellectual profile that S. L. Reames, a modern historian of the *Golden Legend*, extracts from a thorough analysis of his sermons:

> He does not seem to have an appreciation of other perspectives, other value systems, besides the essentially monastic one he celebrates. . . . He also lacks empathy with Christians who must live in the world and with weaker souls who care about earthly blessings. . . . Even his model sermons, which are less extreme than the *Legenda* in most respects, exhibit a noticeable disregard for the everyday needs and concerns of the laity who would hear them. This characteristic of Jacobus' work becomes more understandable when one recalls that he cannot have seen very much of the world before he renounced it in 1244, at the age of fourteen or thereabouts. And the increasingly militant stance of the order in the ensuing years was hardly calculated to sway a young convert towards open-mindedness.[58]

His spirituality can seem harsh to modern readers. The image of God as a loving, accessible Father did not play any role in his works and probably did not figure prominently in his spiritual outlook either. As S. L. Reames says,

> His theological imagination appears to have been adversarial and puritan rather than inclusive and humanistic. Perhaps the most telling evidence in this regard is his tendency to equate sanctity with isolation, joylessness, virtual sterility, and contempt for the values of lesser men.[59]

Nevertheless, the fact that of all eleven Latin versions of the legend, Jacobus's

---

55. Reames (1985) 25.
56. Reames (1985) 3–4.
57. Ryan (1993) xv.
58. Reames (1985) 194.
59. Reames (1985) 195.

was the most read and the most enjoyed for many centuries by those who understood Latin demonstrates his skill to select material that would appeal to a broad spectrum of tastes. Throughout the *Legenda*, his intent was "to humanize and dramatize the doctrinal point made."[60] This was the approach that he took to the abridgement of the legend of Saints Barlaam and Josaphat as well.

2.3. JACOBUS DE VORAGINE IN THE TRANSMISSION CHAIN OF BARLAAM AND JOSAPHAT'S LEGEND

In the process of "humanizing and dramatizing" the legend, Jacobus excised the lengthy theological debates that were the distinct characteristic of the Greek version and that were left intact in the unabridged Latin versions. His aim was to create a vivid narrative, which would resonate with his readers because of its exotic setting, the dramatic conversion story of an Indian prince, and the drama of the clash between a pagan father and a Christian son who successfully cuts through many lies, resists sexual temptations, and converts both his father and his entire Indian kingdom from idol-worship to Christianity.

By taking the lengthy theological debates out and putting the parables of the hermit Barlaam at the core of his version, Jacobus weakened the emphasis on Christian dogma as conveyed through the theological treatises in the unabridged versions. He even omitted the parable of the Sower,[61] the only parable of Christian origin that the unabridged Latin versions include.[62] As a result, the ethical and philosophical messages in the most ancient layers of the legend receive greater prominence.

Jacobus no doubt followed the earlier Christianized versions of the legend. The heroic Buddha, who experiences a life-transforming insight about the inevitability of recurring suffering and transcends it in the attainment of enlightenment under the sacred Bodhi tree, yields place to the Christian Saint Josaphat, who submits to the word of God coming to him through his teacher Barlaam. He does not seek out the teacher; the teacher comes to him when the reality of suffering and death awakens his spiritual yearning. Yet, Jacobus's Josaphat "has some of the subjectivity and initiative of a hero" and "has more individuality than the typical saint in the *Golden Legend*."[63] Josaphat both engages in action and cultivates receptivity to God, so he has the qualities of both a hero and a saint.[64] The defining moment of enlightenment, namely the

---

60. Ryan (1993) xvi.
61. Matthew 13:1–23, Mark 4:1–20, and Luke 8:1–15.
62. Cruz Palma (2001) chapter 39, p. 162.
63. MacQueen (2001) 162.
64. Cf. MacQueen (2001) 161.

complete understanding of "how ignorance leads to suffering and rebirth,"[65] accompanied by the extinction of all attachment and desire is the central event in all the Asian lives of the Buddha. This event was omitted already from the first Christianized version of the legend, the Georgian one. Still, we can detect traces of the heroic Buddha in the Christian Saint Josaphat. Jacobus's abridged version removes some of the layers added to the legend in the process of Christianization and thus foregrounds its oldest strata.

All three episodes from the life of Prince Siddhārtha (Buddha), as told in Asia, receive prominent place in Jacobus's version: the father's consultation with astrologers, the chariot rides, and the sexual temptations.[66] These shared scenes are used, of course, in different ways within the different traditions.[67]

First, both in the life of the Buddha and in the Barlaam and Josaphat legend, the father consults with astrologers about the fate of his newborn son, and the outcomes of this consultation are parallel in both tales.[68] An astrologer predicts that the king's son will become a Buddha; in Jacobus's version the astrologer tells the father, who is an idol-worshipper and persecutor of the Christians, not only that the child will become a Christian one day but that he will reject his father's earthly kingdom in favor of a heavenly one. The father responds in the same way in both versions: he builds an isolated pleasure palace for his son where no one is allowed to mention sickness, old age, suffering, or death to him (chapters 20–27). In Jacobus's version, no one is allowed to mention Christianity to him either.

Second, when the young man grows up, he ventures out on several chariot rides outside the palace and encounters sickness, old age, and death (chapters 48–66). Prince Siddhārtha encounters a mendicant, while Josaphat meets the hermit Barlaam later. In both cases the chariot rides lead to a life-transforming insight about the vanity and unreliability of the physical world. Both protagonists respond by seeking out the causes of suffering and find them in ignorance-fueled desire for the temporary pleasures of the world, leading them to its renunciation. All Christianized versions share with the Buddhist legend a form of ascetic piety that sees the visible world as transitory and unfulfilling. The attitude of weariness with the world is a common trait of medieval Christian and Buddhist sensibilities, as Huizinga already noted at the beginning of the last century.[69]

---

65. Lopez and McCracken (2014) 42.

66. Cf. Lopez (2014) viii, introduction to McCracken's translation of Gui de Cambrai's *Barlaam and Josaphat*.

67. Lopez and McCracken (2014) 220.

68. Lopez and McCracken (2014) 221 conclude that the scene of consultation with astrologers was inserted into the life of the Buddha long before the story made its way to Persia, but it was not part of the original life itself.

69. Huizinga (1996 [1921]) 35, cited in MacQueen (2001) 158.

The Buddha's profound life-transforming realization of the precariousness of the human condition puts him on a long path of harsh self-mortification, which only leads him to the brink of starvation and death. Realizing that this road does not lead to enlightenment and that he may die without attaining his goal, he begs for alms in the nearby village and rebuilds his strength. His companions, the five ascetics, leave him, believing that he has abandoned his commitment to the ascetic endeavor. However, he continues his search and after overcoming all attacks and temptations sent against him by the deity of desire and death, Māra, he awakens, becomes "the awakened one," the Buddha, having attained enlightenment under the sacred Bodhi tree.

As a result, he articulates "the middle way of Buddhism, in this case, the middle way between the extreme of self-indulgence, which he had known as a prince in the palace, and the extreme of self-mortification, which he had known as an ascetic in the wilderness."[70] The enlightenment and the subsequent articulation of the middle way is the Buddha's central insight captured in the four noble truths of Buddhism: "that life is qualified by suffering; that that suffering has a cause; that there is a state of the cessation of suffering called *nirvana* and that there is a path to that state of cessation."[71] Here renunciation is not rejection of the world but the discarding of that which is harmful and obstructive to the attainment of a state beyond suffering and death.

Despite the emphasis on the middle way in the teachings of the Buddha, ascetic piety became over time the most universal theme in the legend:

. . . the values of renunciation, asceticism, and disdain for the world are shared by Buddhists, Muslims, Manicheans, and Christians. The common endorsement of these values explains—at least in part—the broad diffusion of the legend.[72]

The Christian versions likewise emphasize the first two of the noble truths, the understanding of the world as theater of suffering, caused by misdirected desire for the vanity of the world that has to be renounced through the practice of asceticism. They erase the distinct interior event that the lives of the Buddha call "enlightenment."[73] The path to salvation in the Christian versions unfolds in the context of a life-long interaction with a teacher, while the path of the future Buddha is an individual heroic quest. After experiencing the reality of suffering, old age, and death, Prince Josaphat, just like Prince Siddhārtha, is "in

70. Lopez and McCracken (2014) 44.
71. Lopez and McCracken (2014) 44.
72. Pitts, M. B. (1989) *Barlaam et Jozaphas: Roman du XIVe siècle en langue d'Oc*. Paris: Presses de l'Université de Paris 239, cited in Lopez and McCracken (2014) 211.
73. Cf. MacQueen (2001).

great desolation," "thinking over the sights frequently in his heart" (chapter 67).
Unlike Siddārtha, however, who leaves his palace and child behind in search for
enlightenment, Josaphat does not take immediate action. The hermit Barlaam
finds out about his state "through the spirit" (chapter 68) and arrives to offer an
alternative to the disturbing reality that Josaphat has become aware of.

Through long conversations with Barlaam, Josaphat receives confirmation
of his personal insight about the dangers inherent in the world of change and
deceptive appearances, and he learns of the existence of a better, permanent
reality, "God's kingdom." He is not prepared to act upon his initial insight
before the teacher appears. Josaphat's course of learning and instruction
culminates in his conversion to the Christian faith and baptism (chapter 168).
From this point his faith becomes the focus of the narrative. This faith is tested
first intellectually through a theological debate, and eventually through sexual
temptation. In all Christian versions, conversion, baptism, and the triumph
of faith over temptation replace the defining moment of enlightenment,
experienced by the Buddha under the Bodhi tree.[74] While the Buddha "must
demonstrate his enlightenment by liberating other beings from ignorance and
attachment . . . Josaphat must demonstrate his faith in God by passing tests."[75]

The third shared element between the Buddha story and the Barlaam and
Josaphat legend is the episode involving sexual temptation. After witnessing the
disturbing reality of illness, old age, and death, Prince Siddhārtha is unable to
enjoy the pleasures of self-gratification and becomes indifferent to the charms
of attractive women. Prince Siddhārtha's attitude to such temptations "is one of
detached piety rather than of conflicted desire. . . . The women's charms are no
match for his determination; his impassivity is a manifestation of an advanced
spiritual state that allows him to perceive decay and death beneath the women's
beautiful attire."[76] Likewise, Josaphat's father surrounds him with attractive
women in a desperate attempt to wean him away from his desired course of
becoming a Christian monk (chapters 244–261). Unlike Siddhārtha, however,
he is tormented by these temptations (chapters 245–246) and overcomes them
with the help of a divine dream that reveals to him a vision of heaven and hell
(chapters 263–270). It is under the influence of this dream that he succeeds
in overcoming the temptations and in preserving his virginity. Siddhārtha, on
the other hand, to prove his virility and to fulfill his duty to the royal lineage,
fathers a son before leaving the palace in search of enlightenment. He also has
a divine dream, but his dream portends his attainment of enlightenment and it
comes after he makes love to his wife and begets a son.[77]

74. MacQueen (2001) 164.
75. MacQueen (2001) 163.
76. Lopez and McCracken (2014) 29 and 31.
77. Lopez and McCracken (2014) 32.

Josaphat's dream is the closest approximation in the Christian versions to the enlightenment experience in the life of the Buddha. To Josaphat, the dream is an instrument through which he passes the virginity test. It also serves to strengthen his faith. It is not his prime achievement as enlightenment is for the Buddha.[78] Buddha's enlightenment in the Christian versions is replaced by Josaphat's revelations. The dream is a revelation from God, which follows other revelations guiding Josaphat to sainthood. Divine revelation alerts him to the true identity of Nachor disguised as his teacher Barlaam (chapter 174) and this allows him to overcome the first temptation to his faith, an intellectual temptation that plays out as a theological debate between the pagan orators (rhetors) and the astrologer Nachor posing as Barlaam.

Alongside revelation, however, Josaphat's own actions play a key role as well. He acts with astuteness and tact. When he first discovers the shocking realities of old age, suffering, and death in the course of his chariot rides, he wisely disguises his distress and feigns happiness before his father (chapter 67). He also desires eagerly to be "directed and taught" about life's mysteries (chapter 67). He has the patience and insight to receive his future mentor Barlaam, disguised as a merchant, without being deterred by his inferior status and strangeness. He intimidates Nachor who poses as Barlaam (chapters 202–204) and, when assaulted with temptations during the test of virginity, remembers to seek shelter in prayer (262), leading to his transformative dream-vision.

Thus, as MacQueen has noted, Jacobus's Josaphat has the traits of both a hero who acts and a saint who is receptive to divine teaching and revelation.[79] The legend in Jacobus's hands highlights the most ancient and universal layers of the main storyline by retaining Josaphat's initiative and by assigning a significant role to cognition and learning in his path to sainthood. In Jacobus's version, "cognition is in a supportive relationship with faith."[80]

Even though the central attainment of the Buddha, the dramatic enlightenment experience, is missing from the legend of Barlaam and Josaphat, the theme of insight, light, and vision runs as an important thread through the entire narrative: the disturbing sights that Josaphat sees looking out of his chariot (chapters 51–66) become a life-transforming call for action and a profound insight. Without the fictional magic stone that Barlaam uses to gain access to the prince, a stone that would blind anyone who beholds it in the absence of a good moral character and clear vision (chapter 74), two-thirds of the story could not take place. The theme dominates many of the parables where various characters get into trouble for their fascination with deceptive external appearances and their inability to see below the surface of words and

---

78. MacQueen (2001) 162.
79. MacQueen (2001) 161.
80. MacQueen (2001) 164.

events (the four chests, the archer and the nightingale parable, and so on). In the "prince in the cave" parable, a prince is in danger of losing his physical vision. His father saves his eyesight by isolating him in a dark cave for a number of years, but in the end, his infatuation with women, whom he does not even know how to name (chapter 239), deprives him of the clarity of vision and ability to look beyond appearances, qualities that Josaphat exemplifies.

The theme of sight and vision relates to the deeper philosophical insight about the illusory nature of the visible world. The belief in the impermanence and even the nonexistence of the changing everyday world is of Buddhist origin,[81] faithfully preserved in the Christianized versions.[82] It was compatible with Christianity through the familiar passage from Ecclesiastes 12:8 (*Vanity of vanities . . . all is vanity*) and the statement of St Paul "the things which are seen are temporal; but the things which are not seen are eternal" (2 Corinthians 4:18). In this view, all that we see with our physical eyes has no permanent existence, and yet it is an object of misguided desire and short-lived pleasure. All threads of the legend, no matter how loosely connected to the main narrative they might seem, support this theme, beginning with the opening episode, which refers to a time before Josaphat's birth. King Avenir's former friend, a newly converted Christian, informs the king that his two greatest enemies are anger and desire (chapter 9) and that the king needs to discard them. He explains to King Avenir that he chose the ascetic way of life in order to learn how to distinguish the real from the unreal and thus how to cease desiring the unreal:

> Fools despise the things that are real as if they did not exist; on the other hand, they try to comprehend and grasp the things that do not truly exist as if they were real. The person of the sort who has not tasted the sweetness of the things that are real, will not be able to comprehend the truth about[83] the things that have no existence. (chapters 12–14)

The unabridged Latin version of the legend (*Vulgata*) makes very explicit the meaning of "things that do not exist" and contrasts the sweetness of the temporary pleasures with the sweetness of "the things that are real":

> One who has not tasted the sweetness of the things that are real, will not be able to understand the nature of the things that do not exist and will not know how to despise and discard them. The discourse has called real the eternal and unchangeable things. It has called unreal the present

---

81. Cf. Almond (1987) 399.

82. MacQueen (2001) 157.

83. The Georgian version puts it more clearly: "will not be able to cast out" instead of "will not be able to comprehend the truth about. . . ." Cf. Almond (1987) 399.

life, the delights and the false prosperity to which your heart, o king, is unfortunately, severely addicted.[84]

Another friend, a knight who is secretly a Christian, also tries to convert King Avenir with the same message, "recounting the vanities of the world . . ."(chapter 37). So before Barlaam even shows up on the scene, there have been two side episodes that describe failed attempts to convey this message to King Avenir, Josaphat's father. This fact underscores Josaphat's agency, in that unlike his father, he will show remarkable receptivity to this message and will act on it.

Despising temporary pleasures is central to Barlaam's teaching given to Josaphat: "He began to speak against the deceptive pleasures and vanities of the world, adducing many examples in support of this point" (chapter 113). The deluded love for these short-lived pleasures comes alive with the allegory of the man in the well who savors the drops of honey that drip from an upper branch of a tree that he is holding to, forgetting about the mice gnawing at his branch and about the beast beneath waiting to devour him (chapters 113–122). They are also symbolized by the enticing charms of women. Women are invested with a sinister power in the legend and are even called "demons who lead men astray" (chapter 239) because they make men lose power over themselves. Thus women symbolize desire for the world that the legend rejects.

There is an exception to the negative portrayal of women, where a maiden symbolizes the one desire that the legend endorses. This occurs in the episode of the rich youth and the poor maiden (chapters 146–168), Barlaam's last parable that concludes the series of teaching stories addressed to Josaphat. The young man in the parable falls in love with a poor maiden because he sees her as an embodiment of *prudentia*, spiritual wisdom (chapter 153). Similarly, Josaphat falls in love with Barlaam's spiritual wisdom. The wise poor maiden is a symbol of the positive desire for wisdom and self-control.

The Christian adapters strove to Christianize the ancient fables but did not always succeed in doing so seamlessly. For example, the archer and the nightingale parable (chapters 96–112) serves as an illustration of the gullibility of idol-worshippers, but the story can likewise be viewed as an excellent illustration of how the archer's greed and desire for the precious stone clouds his ability to think critically and distinguish reality from falsehood.

The attack on idol-worshippers, artificially tacked onto the archer and the nightingale story, exposes one of the many ironies and paradoxes surrounding this legend.[85] We know today that the fictional character of Josaphat, the enemy of idols, has his origins in the Buddha, who was worshipped as an idol under

---

84. *Vulgata* chapter 12 in Cruz Palma (2001) 118.

85. I am paraphrasing here Lopez (2014) xiv, introduction to McCracken's translation of Gui de Cambrai's *Barlaam and Josaphat*.

many names across many countries and continents. But until the 19th century, the opposite was held true, namely that "Budão (i.e., Buddha) . . . was in fact Josaphat and that over the centuries the people of India had forgotten the true identity of the Christian saint,"[86] as a Portuguese writer of the 16th century claims. There were even attempts to locate in India the palace that King Avenir built for his son.[87]

Today, the legend about Josaphat and his fictional conversion of India to Christianity retains its appeal to a great extent due to the tradition that traces it back to the Buddha. [88] Because of its connection to the life of the founder of a major world religion, it remains an exciting object of study not only for scholars but also for lovers of stories and truths that transcend the confines of cultures and religions.

By transmitting this legend to us in a substantially shortened form and by thus exposing its deepest bedrock of ancient material that was reinterpreted and adapted to many cultural and religious contexts, Jacobus gives the modern reader an opportunity to continue reinterpreting it and to step into the legend's long history of creative transmission.

3. The Context and Storyline of Jacobus de Voragine's Barlaam and Josaphat

The legend consists of a frame narrative with a series of teaching stories or parables embedded into the dialogue between the pious Prince Josaphat and his teacher Barlaam. Just as the entire legend is a parable (*exemplum*) for the edification of the reading or listening audience, the embedded stories are intended to teach not just Josaphat but also various other characters in the story.[89] The teacher Barlaam clearly spells out the allegorical meaning of his parables.

I have divided Jacobus de Voragine's abridged version of the legend into ten parts:

Part 1: Introduction to the characters and the setting.

Parts 2–4: Josaphat faces the facts about the human condition and the problem of the unpredictable and unsatisfactory nature of the world.

Part 5: Barlaam arrives to confirm Josaphat's insight and to orient his

---

86. The quote is by Diogo de Couto cited in Lopez (2014) xiii, introduction to McCracken's translation of Gui de Cambrai's *Barlaam and Josaphat*.

87. Lopez and McCracken (2014) 229.

88. Cf. Lopez (2014) xiv, introduction to McCracken's translation of Gui de Cambrai's *Barlaam and Josaphat*.

89. Bolton (1958) 360.

efforts toward finding a solution. He conveys his teachings in six parables, which take up more than a third of Jacobus's version. At the end of this course of instruction, Josaphat converts to Christianity and is baptized by Barlaam.

Part 6–9: Josaphat's faith is put to two major tests. The first is an intellectual test meant to determine whether he has turned his back on idolatry and whether he can defend his Christian faith before learned pagan orators (rhetors). Divine revelation assists him in passing this test (Parts 6–7). The second test is the test of will where he is subjected to a series of sexual temptations but succeeds in preserving his virginity with the help of a divine dream (Parts 8–9).

Part 10: Josaphat ascends to the throne, then he renounces his kingdom and retreats to the desert where he attains to sainthood.

3.1. THE GENRE

The legend of Barlaam and Josaphat is both hagiography and romance[90] due to its fictional plotline filled with intrigue, suspense, and sexual temptations. Because it focuses on Barlaam's spiritual and moral instruction of Josaphat, the legend also falls within the homiletic tradition, namely it is a public discourse on a religious subject. It contains a dramatic conversion story and strikes the right balance between edification and entertainment, which may have been one of the secrets to its popularity.

3.2. THE SETTING

The fictional life of Barlaam and Josaphat takes place outside of time and place, but most versions mention India in their introductory paragraphs. The other place name they mention is the land of Senaar (chapter 68 in Jacobus's version). Barlaam comes from this land, which the Georgian version identifies with Ceylon,[91] the Greek version—with the land between the Tigris and Euphrates, known then as Chaldea or Babylonia.[92] The Greek version evinces confusion regarding Ethiopia and India, which is typical in medieval Western texts.[93] It introduces the legend in the following way:

> An edifying story from the inner land of the Ethiopians, called the land of the Indians. . . . [94]

---

90. It is called *romanzo* (Italian) by Maggioni (2007) 1707 and *roman* (French) by Sonet (1949). Lang (introduction to Woodward and Mattingly (1997) xxvi) calls it *romance*.

91. Almond (1987) 393.

92. Woodward and Mattingly (1997) 624 (index).

93. Lopez and McCracken (2014) 123.

94. Woodward and Mattingly (1997) 3.

It goes on to describe the location of this land in greater detail:

> The country of the Indians, as it is called, is vast and populous, lying far beyond Egypt. On the side of Egypt, it is washed by seas and navigable gulfs, but on the mainland it marches with the borders of Persia, a land formerly darkened with the gloom of idolatry. . . .[95]

The unabridged Latin versions say that Prince Josaphat was educated "in all the learning of the Ethiopians and the Persians."[96] India does get conflated indeed with Ethiopia.

In terms of time, the Greek version situates the events in the story several centuries after Apostle Thomas converted India to Christianity:

> . . . one of the company of Christ's Twelve Apostles, most holy Thomas, was sent out to the land of the Indians, preaching the Gospel of Salvation.[97]

After the mission of Saint Thomas was complete, India (in this scenario) relapsed into idolatry with the passage of time. A new surge of enthusiasm for ascetic monasticism came about through the inspiring example of the Egyptian Desert Fathers whose fame had reached India. The Greek version states:

> Now when monasteries began to be formed in Egypt, and numbers of monks banded themselves together, and when the fame of their virtues and Angelic conversation "was gone out into all the ends of the world"[98] and came to the Indians, it stirred them up also to the like zeal, insomuch that many of them forsook everything and withdrew to the deserts.[99]

Desert monasticism (4th century CE) was a historical phenomenon that marked the beginning of Christian monasticism in the deserts of Egypt, Palestine, and Syria.[100]

The unabridged Latin version omits much of the background available in the Greek version and begins with the monastic revival *without* mentioning Egypt. Thus it implies that Christian monasticism (unspecified as to location) exerted its influence upon the Indian desert monks:

---

95. Woodward and Mattingly (1997) 7.
96. *Vulgata* chapter 29 in Cruz Palma (2001) 146.
97. Woodward-Mattingly (1997) 9.
98. Language from *Psalm* XIX.4.
99. Woodward-Mattingly (1997) 9.
100. For more on the Desert Fathers, cf. Harmless (2004) *passim* and on Mothers *ibidem* 440 ff.

> When monasteries began to be built and multitudes of monks began to
> gather and the blessed rumor about their fame and angelic conversation
> filled the world and reached to the Indians, it inspired them to a similar zeal
> such that many of them abandoned everything and sought the deserts and
> while in a mortal body, began associating with the angels.[101]

Jacobus de Voragine begins abruptly with no mention of the external influences
that sparked the surge of monastic zeal in India. He introduces king Avenir
right away:

> When all of India was full of Christians and monks, a certain very powerful
> king rose to power, called Avenir who intensely persecuted the Christians
> and especially all the monks. (chapter 2)

Although Jacobus left out most details about background from the beginning
of his abridged version, he still linked the legend to desert monasticism. At
the end of his version of the legend (chapter 290), he gives a date for the death
of Barlaam, which is absent from all earlier versions and which he evidently
invented. Even Vincent de Beauvais did not venture a date in his encyclopedic
entry on the two saints. Jacobus gives the fictional date of 380 CE as the year of
the death of Josaphat's teacher, thus closely associating Barlaam with the time
period of the Desert Fathers. Anthony the Great, saint and model for desert
asceticism, died in 356 CE, about twenty-five years before the alleged date of
the death of Barlaam.

In all Christianized versions of the legend, there is one main obstacle that
prevents India from adopting Christianity despite the vigorous monastic revival
mentioned at the beginning of the narrative. This obstacle is King Avenir, who
worships idols, lives in enjoyment of royal luxury, and therefore persecutes the
monastics in his kingdom. King Avenir is the focus of attention from the start
of Jacobus's version of the legend.

3.3. THE STORYLINE

Part 1: King Avenir Encounters Christianity at His Own Court (2–18)

Even though the King persecutes the monks, the irresistible attraction of the
monastic way of life makes a convert out of one of his friends, a nobleman who
gives up his luxurious lifestyle and retreats to the desert. The king captures
him and brings him back. A short exchange follows in which the friend, now
monk, identifies anger and desire as the king's greatest enemies. The king has to

---

101. My translation from the Latin of the unabridged version (*Vulgata*) in de la Cruz Palma
(2001) 108.

give those up temporarily in order to enter into a debate with him. The debate ends with the king expelling the nobleman. Having hoped to provoke the king's anger, to be killed by him, and thus to become a martyr for his faith, the Christian nobleman departs disappointed. During this encounter, King Avenir learns about the faith that one day his yet-unborn son will embrace.

Part 2: The Birth of Prince Josaphat (19–27)

A son is born to King Avenir whom he names Josaphat. An astrologer predicts that the young prince will become devoted to the Christian religion and will exchange his earthly kingdom for a heavenly one (23). The alarmed Avenir builds a remote pleasure palace for his son to prevent this from happening. He thinks that if his son lives surrounded by pleasures that would keep him happy, he will not be inclined to leave his comfortable palace and pursue the ascetic life of a poor monk. The king brings him up there in an artificial environment that shields the child from witnessing pain, sickness, old age, and death.

Part 3: The Christian Knight and the Word-Mender (28–47)

This episode is loosely linked to the rest of the narrative and appears to be a digression showing the ubiquitous appeal of Christianity that keeps infiltrating Avenir's palace. However, it sets up a major theme within the legend, that of "the conflict between loyalty to an earthly king and obedience to a spiritual lord" and is probably based upon an Arabic tale.[102] It illustrates the rewarding nature of charity and the admirable quality of handling difficult situations and fake narratives with tact and wit.

A certain knight (anonymous) enjoyed King Avenir's respect and friendship. However, since he was secretly Christian and he had to carefully hide his religious leanings in view of Avenir's hostility toward this religion. One day, out of kindness, he offered hospitality to a self-proclaimed "word-mender," a "doctor of words," and helped him recover from his wounds received in a hunting accident. This will be the reader's first encounter with the intricate net of deceptions, pretenses, and fake narratives that permeate this legend. In a conversation with the knight, the king pretends to be interested in Christianity to test the knight's reaction to this feigned change of heart. The knight naïvely falls into the king's trap. The "word-mender" saves the knight with advice on how to extricate himself from the complicated intrigues of the jealous courtiers who had set this trap for him, trying to trick him into confessing his Christianity to the king and thus losing his excellent standing in the court hierarchy.

The knight hides his Christianity just as Josaphat will have to hide his. The

---

102. Lopez and McCracken (2014) 64.

conflict between duty to his royal father Avenir and attraction to his spiritual father Barlaam encapsulates Josaphat's predicament throughout the legend and this predicament is foreshadowed in this episode.

Part 4: Prince Josaphat's Chariot Rides (48–66)

We are now back in the main storyline. Josaphat is confronted with the reality of pain, illness, old age, and death when he encounters a leper, a blind man, and an old man during his chariot rides outside his palace. He is shocked by these discoveries and eager to learn more about the mortal condition, but he wisely disguises his feelings and feigns happiness before his father. Josaphat does not only make these discoveries but also desires to learn their cause. The witnessing of suffering and death is not simply a shocking experience for him, but a life-transforming revelation. He perceives it as a sign that awakens in him the desire to "be directed and taught," namely he becomes a seeker. This turns his otherwise unremarkable discovery into an insight that determines the course of the rest of his life.

Part 5: Barlaam Arrives and Starts to Instruct Prince Josaphat (67–76)

Barlaam, disguised as merchant, arrives at the palace of the prince and seeks audience with him. He gains admittance under the pretext that he has a magic stone, which can give sight to the blind, hearing to the deaf, voice to the dumb, and wisdom to fools. Since the stone is metaphorical and he cannot show it to Josaphat's current tutor, who demands to see it in order to give him access to the prince, Barlaam adds another property to the other magic qualities of the stone: it would blind anyone whose eyes and character are not pure, if that person were to look at it. Conscious of his impure character, the tutor loses interest in seeing the stone and grants Barlaam admission to the prince. The "magic stone" stands for Barlaam's teaching, which is not meant for everyone but only for the prince, who is in a receptive state of mind. His conversion will cure his spiritual sight, deafness, and lack of wisdom.

5.1. Barlaam's First Parable: The Herald of Death and the Four Chests (77–95)

Barlaam uses this parable to compliment Josaphat for admitting him and listening to him despite his lower status and inability to produce a visible "magic stone." With his first parable, he gives the prince two allegorical lessons in the value of distinguishing between outer appearance and inner reality. The king in Barlaam's parable is god-fearing and respectful toward people of lower status.

He bows before some unkempt poor persons (probably monks). Because his brother and his courtiers reproach him for that, he teaches them two practical lessons about the deceptive nature of appearances.

The first practical lesson involves a herald of death. The king decides to scare his brother into believing that he wishes to execute him, a variation on an ancient story attested in the lore around the Indian King Aśoka.[103]

The fable of the four chests is the second practical lesson. The courtiers are asked to choose from four chests, some covered with pitch but containing gems and pearls, and the others covered with gold but containing rot.

The brother reads the herald of death literally rather than figuratively. He is foolish to take at face value the message of the herald, sent by his own brother whom he had not offended, while berating the king for fearing the symbolic heralds of God, namely the poor monks; the courtiers who only see the surface of the gilded chests are made to look like those chests, glittering on the outside but rotten on the inside. The poor monks, on the other hand, whose appearance is homely, are full of inner riches.

5.2. Barlaam's Second Parable: The Archer and the Nightingale (96–112)

The Christianization of the legend, which started with the Georgian version, is far from seamless. Some parables are artificially harnessed to a specific ideological agenda, which does not sit well with the original story. The incongruity between the frame narrative and the ancient folk-stories that fill it is best exemplified by the fable of the archer and the nightingale. The parable is supposed to illustrate the gullibility of idol-worshippers, but actually it illustrates the archer's lack of critical thinking caused by greed. Through contrast, it aims to show the opposite side of an important theme in the legend: the ability to distinguish true from false, real from fake.

An archer captures a nightingale that talks to him, promising to give him three useful mandates if he lets it go. When the bird regains its freedom, the archer receives three basic maxims: do not try to get something that is beyond your reach; do not cry over spilt milk; if something sounds too good, do not trust it. The bird then presents a series of false claims to the archer, but he fails to see through the nightingale's lies. By being unable to understand and apply the nightingale's three basic maxims, the gullible archer remains empty-handed. He turns into a cautionary tale that illustrates the plight of any person who loses the ability to think critically under the influence of greed rather than the gullibility of idol-worshippers specifically.

---

103. Lopez and McCracken (2014) 223; cf. Almond (1987) 398.

5.3. Barlaam's Third Parable: The Man in the Well (113–122)

This parable is an allegorical representation of human life. It was quite popular long before Jacobus included it in his legend. An illustration of it appears above the south portal of the Baptistery in Parma, some 140 miles east of Jacobus's birthplace, Varazze (see fig. 1). The carved relief is the work of an artist who died in the same year in which Jacobus was born.

The allegory is meant to illustrate the condition of those who are thoughtlessly immersed in the sweetness of transitory pleasures. They are compared to a man who was chased by a unicorn symbolizing Death. While trying to escape, he fell into a deep well. There he landed on a platform consisting of four vipers (asps); while holding onto two branches with his hands, he noticed that those branches were being eaten away by a black mouse and a white mouse, symbols of night and day, constantly cutting his life shorter. Looking down, he saw a dragon with an open mouth, waiting to devour him. However, he noticed a drip of honey trickling down from above and enticed by its sweetness, forgot about the predicament he was in. With this parable, Barlaam vividly illustrates the precariousness of the human condition, which human beings, blinded by the sweetness of temporary pleasures, ignore. The allegory is included in the Indian *Mahābhārata*[104] and *Pantschatantra*[105] as well as in Jain writings.[106] This means that the tale predates Buddhism and that Buddhists themselves incorporated the fable into the story of their savior from an earlier Hindu or Jain source.[107]

Figure 1 shows the earliest sculpted version of the parable about the man in the well.[108] The choice of this theme is unusual in the context of the sculptures on the other portals that represent the Virgin (north) and the Last Judgment (west).[109] The personifications of the sun and the moon appear on the left and the right of the tree that symbolizes human life, first on a chariot and again above each chariot. The sun and the moon are common in ancient Roman monuments, as for example on the arch of Constantine.[110] However, for those familiar with the Barlaam and Josaphat legend, the sun and the moon on both sides of the tree support the symbolism of the black and white mice gnawing at the roots of the tree. As the mice in the parable, so also the sun and the moon, added by the artist, stand for the passage of day and night that are cutting human life shorter with each passing day.

---

104. Lopez and McCracken (2014) 100.
105. Almond (1987) 395.
106. Almond (1987) 398.
107. Cf. Smith (1981) 9.
108. Glass (2015) 277.
109. Glass (2015) 256.
110. Glass (2015) 280.

Fig. 1. Antelami, Benedetto (fl. 1150–c. 1230). Legend of Barlaam and Josaphat. Romanesque. Relief on the tympanon of the south portal of the Baptistery, Parma, Italy.
Photo courtesy Scala/ Art Resource, NY.

5.4. Barlaam's Fourth Parable: The Man and His Three Friends (123–138)

The value of kindness, friendship, and compassion is the focus of this parable, which illustrates the unreliable and transitory companionship of wealth and family, as well as the lasting companionship of trust, hope, and charity.

5.5. Barlaam's Fifth Parable: The King for One Year (139–145)

The value of charity and building treasures in heaven (Matthew 6:19–21) is the exclusive focus of this parable about a man who arrived to a town that had strange customs. The citizens would enthrone a visiting stranger and make him a king for a year, but after the year was over they would banish him to a deserted island where he would suffer from hunger and cold. However, the man in the parable learns of this custom and plans ahead by sending treasures and supplies to that island during the time when he is still king. The meaning of the parable is that while one can take nothing with oneself to the other world, one can send ahead riches for oneself to the beyond through "the hands of the poor."

This parable has a strong Christian overtone, but it is also found in the Arabic version that may have received it from the Buddhist source.[111]

5.6. Barlaam's Sixth Parable: The Rich Youth and the Poor Maiden. Josaphat Receives Baptism (146–168)

After hearing these inspiring illustrations, Josaphat wants to follow Barlaam into the desert immediately. Barlaam cautions him against such a hasty action, which would only enrage the king and provoke him to persecute the monks more fiercely. However, he encourages Josaphat's resolve with a parable of a noble youth who, just like Josaphat, learned to look beyond appearances and to prefer lasting inner virtues to transitory superficial advantages.

The youth in Barlaam's parable refuses to marry the rich bride that his father has chosen for him. He meets a poor maiden who works hard and at the same time praises God with gratitude for all the gifts he has bestowed upon her. The youth falls in love with her because of her *prudentia*, spiritual wisdom, and asks to marry her, but her father refuses to let her go, demanding that the youth live with the family in their poor hut. The youth agrees and later discovers that her father is actually very rich.

The youth in the parable mirrors Josaphat who had fallen in love with spiritual wisdom, symbolized by the poor maiden, the embodiment of wisdom in the parable. The rich bride that the youth rejected is the kingdom that Josaphat will reject for a more lasting one that he will pursue through the inconspicuous life of a desert hermit. After baptizing Josaphat, Barlaam disappears into the desert.

Part 6: King Avenir's Effort to Bring the Prince Back to Idol-Worship with the Help of Fake Barlaam (169–192)

Enraged by the news of his son's baptism, King Avenir tries to reason with his son, but to no avail. Thus, he takes advice from a friend, called Arachis, to resort to a deceptive scheme that includes a fake Barlaam. This Barlaam in disguise is actually the pagan priest Nachor, the teacher of Arachis. The king will stage a theological debate between disguised Barlaam (Nachor) and the orators at his court (rhetors). The desired outcome of the debate is this: Nachor would let himself be defeated; the defeat would publicly discredit Barlaam and his Christianity; as a result, Prince Josaphat, disappointed with Barlaam, would return to idolatry.

---

111. Lopez and McCracken (2014) 224

Part 7: The Debate between Fake Barlaam (Nachor) and the Pagan Orators (193–229)

Through divine revelation (chapter 174), Prince Josaphat has already discovered the deception and has realized that Nachor disguised as Barlaam was not his teacher. He threatens Nachor with punishment and death if he does not win the debate. Nachor, caught between a rock and a hard place, masterfully defends Christianity and wins the debate. Jacobus compresses Nachor's defense of Christianity into six sentences (chapters 213–219). The same defense (Greek *apologia*) takes eight pages in the unabridged Latin version. This defense, coming from the mouth of a pagan magus, is an important historical source inserted into the legend. It is now dated to 125 CE and is known as the *Apology of Aristides* because the philosopher Aristides, a convert to Christianity, delivered it before Emperor Hadrian in Athens (see the commentary to these chapters). The double identity of Aristides, who continued to wear his philosopher's robes after his conversion,[112] matches well the double identity of Nachor disguised as Barlaam.

The king is furious at the collapse of his scheme and dismisses the public debate, but allows Nachor, still disguised as Barlaam, to stay with Josaphat. Josaphat discloses to Nachor his knowledge of Nachor's true identity and converts him to Christianity. Nachor takes up the monastic vocation after his conversion.

Part 8: The Prince in the Cave Allegory and Josaphat's Sexual Temptations (230–261)

The magician Theodas approaches the exasperated and furious king with another plan to divert Josaphat from the ascetic way of life. He suggests filling the palace with seductive women who will surely tempt the prince. He illustrates his point with a fable, the last one in Jacobus's version of the legend and the only one not spoken by Barlaam. The message of this fable negates Barlaam's parables in that it illustrates the irresistible power of sexual desire that transcends language. The fable celebrates the power of seductive appearance and the impossibility to shield oneself from it.

Theodas's fable is Josaphat's life-story turned upside down. In it, there is a prince who had to spend the first ten years of his life in a dark cave, for he was fated to lose his eyesight if he were to see the sun before that. When the prince reached an age when it was safe for him to see the sun, he started learning the names of things. Someone jokingly told him that the name of women is

---

112. Lopez and McCracken (2014) 134.

"demons who lead men astray," and when his father asked what he liked best from the things seen during the day, the prince responded that the "demons who lead men astray" excited him the most. The prince in the fable serves as a foil to Josaphat. While he is entirely literal-minded and enthusiastically chooses the love of the senses, Josaphat will look for a reality and joy deeper than the instant gratification of the physical senses.

At this point it is not Josaphat's Christianity that is under attack but his extreme practice of it, namely sexual abstinence and the observance of celibacy. A beautiful orphan princess comes close to swaying Josaphat to have sex with her. She inflames him with passion and argues that Christians are allowed to have wives. She says that she would convert to Christianity if the prince sleeps with her and thus he will gain merit in heaven for converting a sinner (chapters 251–257).

Part 9: Josaphat's Divine Dream and King Avenir's Conversion (262–277)

Josaphat seeks comfort in prayer and a divine dream saves him from the temptations. In the dream, he sees the delights of heaven and the disgusting corners of hell. When he awakens, both the beautiful princess and the other women sent to tempt him appear repulsive to him. In an unexpected turn of events, Josaphat converts the magus Theodas to Christianity as well. King Avenir admits defeat and upon the advice of his friends yields half of his kingdom to his son, who builds churches and monasteries on his portion of the territory.

Part 10: Josaphat Becomes a Saint (278–292)

King Avenir himself also converts to Christianity and dies peacefully. Josaphat now sees an opportunity to fulfill his dream of withdrawing to the desert. He appoints a loyal friend Barachias to govern the entire kingdom and puts on the habit of a monk. He spends a life of struggle, battling the devil, but is eventually reunited with his teacher Barlaam. Following the death of his teacher, he continues his ascetic feats in the desert and attains sainthood. Eventually, he is buried in the same tomb where Barlaam rests. Miracles happen around the burial site of the two saints and Barachias transfers their remains to his capital city.

The ending contains many details that were first added to the Greek version: the fact that Josaphat was twenty-five when he renounced his kingdom, that he spent thirty-five years in the desert, that he was buried next to his teacher Barlaam, that their remains were transferred to the capital city, and that many miracles happened around their tomb. Since medieval audiences had a distinct taste for narratives about intense struggles for the attainment of sainthood and for miracles surrounding past saints, the elaborate ending was among the factors that contributed to the enduring popularity of the legend in subsequent centuries.[113]

Bibliography

The Latin text used in this commentary was taken from:

Iacopo da Varazze, *Legenda aurea, con le miniature dal codice Ambrosiano C 240 inf.*
Testo critico riveduto e commento a cura di Giovanni Paolo Maggioni.
Traduzione italiana coordinata da Francesco Stella
Edizione Nazionale dei testi mediolatini, 20 (2 voll.)
Firenze, SISMEL—Edizioni del Galluzzo, 2007
ISBN: 978-88-8450-245-2 (paperback edition)
(© Edizione Nazionale dei testi mediolatini, © SISMEL—Edizioni del Galluzzo.
Per le immagini © Biblioteca Ambrosiana)

The complete translation of the legend (the Vulgata*) from Greek into Latin can be consulted in:*

Cruz Palma, Óscar de la (2001). *Barlaam et Iosaphat, version vulgata latina con la traduccion castellana de Juan de Arce Solorceno* (1608). Madrid, Bellaterra: Consejo Superior de Investigatciones Cientificas. Universitat Autonoma de Barcelona. Servei de Publicacions (Nueva Roma 12).

Pedagogy, background, and textual tradition:

Aavitsland, K. B. (2012). *Imagining the Human Condition in Medieval Rome: The Cistercian Fresco Cycle at Abbazia delle Tre Fontane.* Surrey, England; Burlington, VT: Ashgate Publishing.
Almond, P. (1987). "The Buddha of Christendom: A Review of the Legend of Barlaam and Josaphat," *Religious Studies* 23: 391–406.
Bolton, W. F. (1958). "Parable, Allegory and Romance in the Legend of Barlaam and Josaphat," *Traditio* 14: 359–66.
Clark, J. R. (1979). "Teaching Medieval Latin," *The Classical Journal* 75: 44–50.
Diels, H., and W. Kranz (1966). *Die Fragmente der Vorsokratiker*, vol. 1. Dublin and Zürich: Weidmann.
Glass, D. F. (2015). "The Sculpture of the Baptistery of Parma: Context and Meaning," *Mitteilungen des Kunsthistorischen Institutes in Florenz* 57.3: 255–93.

---

113. Lopez and McCracken (2014) 136.

Godfrey, A. W. (2003). *Medieval Mosaic*. Wauconda, IL: Bolchazy-Carducci.

Gupta, B. (2012). *An Introduction to Indian Philosophy: Perspectives on Reality, Knowledge and Freedom*. New York: Routledge.

Huizinga, J. (1996 [1921]). *The Autumn of the Middle Ages*. Chicago: University of Chicago Press.

Kenoyer, J. M. (1998). *Ancient Cities of the Indus Valley Civilization*. Oxford: Oxford University Press.

Lang, D. M., tr. (1966). *The Balavariani*. Cambridge: Cambridge University Press.

Lang, D. M. (1958). *The Wisdom of Balahvar: A Christian Legend of the Buddha*. London: George Allen and Unwin.

Lanham, C. D. (1975). "The Bastard at the Family Reunion: Classics and Medieval Latin," *The Classical Journal* 70: 46–59.

Lanham, C. D. (1980) "More on Teaching Medieval Latin," *The Classical Journal* 75: 335–39.

Lopez, D. S., and P. McCracken (2014). *In Search of the Christian Buddha: How an Asian Sage Became a Medieval Saint*. New York and London: W. W. Norton.

MacQueen, G. (2001). "Rejecting Enlightenment? The Medieval Christian Transformation of the Buddha-Legend in Jacobus de Voragine's *Barlaam and Josaphat*." *Studies in Religion/Sciences Religieuses* 30.2: 151–65.

McCracken, Peggy, tr., and D. S. Lopez (introduction) and Guy de Cambrai (2014). *Barlaam and Josaphat: A Christian Tale of the Buddha*. New York: Penguin Books (Penguin Classics).

Ryan, W. G., tr., and Jacobus de Voragine (1993). *The Golden Legend: Readings on the Saints*, vols. 1–2. Princeton: Princeton University Press.

Smith, W. C. (1981). *Towards a World Theology: Faith and the Comparative History of Religion*. London and Basingstoke: Macmillan Press.

Sonet, S. J. (1949). *Le roman de Barlaam et Josaphat*. Tome 1: *Recherches sur la tradition manuscrite latine et française*. Namur, Bibliothèque de la Fac. de Phil. et Lettres.

Spevak, O. (2014). *The Noun Phrase in Classical Latin Prose*. Amsterdam Studies in Classical Philology, vol. 21. Leiden and Boston: Brill.

Vincent de Beauvais (1964). *Bibliotheca mundi. Speculum quadruplex sive Speculum majus: naturale, doctrinale, morale, historiale*, vols. 1–4. Duaci: ex officina typographica Baltazaris Belleri 1624. Graz, Austria: Akademische Druck- und Verlagsanstalt.

Works used in the Commentary and Grammar section:

Adams, J. N. (2011). "Late Latin," in J. Clackson, ed., *A Companion to the Latin Language*. Malden, MA: Wiley- Blackwell. 257–83.

Dinkova-Brunn, G. (2011). "Medieval Latin," in J. Clackson, ed., *A Companion to the Latin Language*. Malden, MA: Wiley-Blackwell. 284–302.

Elliott, A. G. (1997). "A Brief Introduction to Medieval Latin Grammar," in K. P. Harrington, ed. (revised by J. Pucci), *Medieval Latin*, 2nd ed. Chicago and London: Chicago University Press. 1–51.

Greenough, J. B., G. L. Kittredge, A. A. Howard, and Benjamin L. D'Ooge, eds. (2003). *Allen and Greenough's New Latin Grammar for Schools and Colleges.* Updated for Focus by Anne Mahoney. Newburyport, MA: Focus Publishing.

Hofmann, J. B., and A. Szantyr (1972). *Lateinische Syntax und Stilistik.* Münhen: C. H. Beck.

Niermeyer, J. F. (1954). *Mediae Latinitatis lexicon minus. A Medieval Latin– French/English Dictionary.* Perficiendum curavit C. van de Kleft. Leiden: Brill.

Norberg, D. L. (1968). *Manuel pratique de latin médiéval.* Paris: J. &A. Picard.

Rigg, A. G. (1996). "Morphology and Syntax," in F. A. C. Mantello and A. G. Rigg, eds., *Medieval Latin: An Introduction and Bibliographical Guide.* Washington, DC: Catholic University of America Press. 83–92.

Shelmerdine, S. C. (2013). *Introduction to Latin.* Newburyport, MA: Focus Publishing.

Sidwell, K. (1995). *Reading Medieval Latin.* Cambridge: Cambridge University Press.

Souter, A. (1996). *A Glossary of Later Latin to 600 A.D.* Oxford: Clarendon Press.

Stotz, P. (1996–2004). *Handbuch zur lateinischen Sprache des Mittelalters.* Munich: Beck. Vv.1–5.

Text with
Medieval Latin
Orthography

Text with Medieval Latin Orthography

1 Barlaam, cuius hystoriam Iohannes Damascenus diligenti studio compilauit, operante in eo diuina gratia sanctum Iosaphat regem ad fidem conuertit.

Part 1: *King Avenir Encounters Christianity at His Own Court*

2 Etenim cum uniuersa India christianis et monachis plena esset, surrexit rex quidam prepotens nomine Auenir qui christianos et precipue monachos plurimum persequebatur. 3 Accidit autem ut quidam regis amicus et in palatio suo primus diuina commotus gratia regiam aulam relinqueret et monasticum ordinem introiret. 4 Quod rex audiens et pre ira insaniens eum per queque deserta inquiri fecit et uix inuentum ad se adduci mandauit. 5 Videnesque eum uili tunica coopertum et fame maceratum, qui splendidis uestimentis ornabatur et multis deliciis affluere consueuerat, dixit ei: 6 "O stulte ac mentis perdite, cur honorem in contumeliam commutasti et te ludum puerorum fecisti?" 7 Cui ille: "Si huius a me rationem audire desideras inimicos tuos a te procul abicias." 8 Rege autem qui essent huius inimici querente, ait: 9 "Ira et concupiscentia. Hec enim impediunt ne ueritas uideatur. 10 Assideant autem ad audentiam dicendorum prudentia et equitas." 11 Cui rex: "Fiat ut loqueris." 12 Et ille: "Insipientes ea que sunt despiciunt quasi non sint; 13 que uero non sunt quasi sint apprehendere moliuntur. 14 Qui autem non gustauerit eorum que sunt dulcedinem, non poterit eorum que non sunt addiscere ueritatem." 15 Multa autem illo de misterio incarnationis et fidei prosequente, rex ait: 16 "Nisi tibi in principio promisissem quod de medio concilii iram remouerem, nunc utique igni tuas carnes traderem. 17 Surge igitur et fuge ex oculis meis ne ultra te uideam et male te perdam." 18 Vir autem dei tristis abscessit eo quod martyrium perpessus non esset.

Part 2: The Birth of Prince Josaphat

19 Interea, dum rex liberos non haberet, puer ei pulcherrimus nascitur et Iosaphat appellatur. **20** Congregante autem rege infinitam multitudinem ut diis pro ortu pueri immolarent, LV astrologos connuocauit, a quibus quid futurum esset filio suo diligenter quesiuit. **21** Cunctis autem respondentibus eum magnum in diuitiis et potentia futurum, unus sapientior ex ipsis dixit: **22** "Puer iste qui natus est tibi, o rex, non in tuo erit regno, sed in alio incomparabiliter meliori. **23** Nam illius quam persequeris christiane religionis, ut estimo, futurus est cultor." **24** Hoc autem non a semet ipso, sed a deo inspirante dixit. **25** Audiens hoc rex et plurimum expauescens in ciuitate seorsum palatium speciosissimum construi fecit et ibi puerum ad habitandum posuit ibique secum iuuenes pulcherrimos collocauit, **26** precipiens illis ut nec mortem nec senectutem nec infirmitatem uel paupertatem nec aliquid quod possit afferre tristitiam sibi ei nominarent, sed omnia iucunda ei proponerent, quatenus mens eius letitiis occupata nihil de futuris cogitare posset. **27** Si quem uero ministrantium infirmari contingeret, hunc protinus rex precipiebat eici et alium loco eius incolumem subrogari, precepitque ne sibi de Christo aliquam facerent mentionem.

Part 3: The Christian Knight and the Word-Mender

28 Eodem tempore erat cum rege uir quidam christianissimus sed occultus qui inter nobiles regis principes primus erat. **29** Hic dum aliquando cum rege ad uenandum iuisset, hominem quendam pauperem pedem lesum a bestia habentem et in terra iacentem inuenit, a quo rogatur ut se suscipere debeat quia sibi in aliquo forsitan prodesse posset. **30** Cui miles: "Ego quidem te libenter suscipio, sed in quo utilis inueniaris ignoro." **31** Et ille dixit: **32** "Ego homo sum medicus uerborum. **33** Si enim aliquis in uerbis ledatur, congruam scio adhibere medelam." **34** Miles autem quod ille dicebat pro nihilo computauit, propter deum tamen eum suscipiens eius curam egit. **35** Viri autem quidam inuidi et malitiosi uidentes predictum principem in tantam gratiam regis esse ipsum apud regem accusauerunt quod non solum ad christianorum fidem declinasset, sed insuper regnum sibi conabatur subripere turbam sollicitans et sibi concilians. **36** "Sed si hoc," inquiunt, "ita esse, o rex, scire desideras, ipsum secreto aduoca et uitam hanc cito finiendam commemora et idcirco gloriam regni te uelle derelinquere et monachorum habitum assumere asseras quos tamen ignoranter hactenus fueras persecutus et tunc uidebis quid tibi responderit." **37** Que cum rex omnia ut illi suaserant fecisset, ille doli ignarus perfusus lacrimis propositum regis laudauit et uanitatem mundi rememorans quantocius hoc adimplendum consuluit. **38** Quod rex audiens et uerum esse quod illi dixerant credens, furore repletus est, nihil tamen sibi respondit. **39** Vir autem perpendens quod rex grauiter uerba sua acceperat, tremens abscessit et medicum se habere uerborum recolens omnia sibi narrauit. **40** Cui ille: "Notum tibi sit quod rex suspicatur ut propter hoc dixeris quod eius regnum uelis inuadere. **41** Surge igitur et comam tuam tonde et uestimenta abiciens cilicium indue et summo diluculo ad regem ingredere. **42** Cumque rex quid sibi hoc uelit interrogauerit, respondebis: **43** "Ecce rex, paratus sum sequi te. **44** Nam etsi uia per quam cupis ire difficilis sit, tecum tamen existenti facilis mihi erit. **45** Sicut enim me socium habuisti in prosperis, sic habebis pariter in aduersis. **46** Nunc igitur presto sum, quid moraris?" "**47** Quod cum ille per ordinem fecisset, rex obstupuit et falsarios arguens uirum ampliori honore dotauit.

Part 4: Prince Josaphat's Chariot Rides

48 Filius igitur eius in palatio educatus ad etatem adultam peruenit et in omni sapientia plene edoctus fuit. **49** Admirans igitur cur pater sic eum reclusisset, unum de conseruis sibi familiariorem secreto de hac re interrogauit, dicens se in multa mestitia positum pro eo quod sibi foras egredi non liceret adeo ut nec cibus sibi saperet nec potus. **50** Quod pater audiens et dolens, equos idoneos parari fecit et choros plaudentes ante eum mittens, ne quid sibi fedum occurreret diligenter prohibuit. **51** Predicto igitur iuuene taliter procedente, quadam uice unus leprosus et unus cecus sibi obuiauerunt. **52** Quos ille uidens et stupens, qui sint et quidnam habeant inquisiuit et ministri dixerunt: **53** "Passiones iste sunt que hominibus accidunt." **54** Et ille: "Omnibus hominibus hec contingere solent?" **55** Negantibus illis respondit: **56** "Noti sunt igitur qui hoc pati debeant an sic indefinite proueniunt?" **57** Et illi: "Et quis hominum futura scire ualet?" **58** Valde igitur anxius esse cepit pro inconsuetudine rei. **59** Alia autem uice quendam ualde senem rugosam habentem faciem et dorsum incuruatum et cadentibus dentibus balbutiendo loquentem inuenit. **60** Stupefactus discere cupit uisionis miraculum cumque didicisset quod propter annorum multitudinem ad talem statum uenisset, ait: **61** "Et quis est huius finis?" **62** Dicunt ei: "Mors." **63** Et ille: "Estne mors omnium uel aliquorum?" **64** Cumque didicisset omnes mori debere, interrogauit: **65** "In quot annis hec superueniunt?" **66** Et illi: "In octoginta uel centum annis senectus inducitur, deinde mors ipsa subsequitur."

Part 5: Barlaam Arrives and Starts to Instruct Prince Josaphat

67 Hec igitur iuuenis frequenter in corde suo recogitans in multa desolatione erat, sed coram patre letitiam pretendebat, plurimum desiderans in huiusmodi dirigi et doceri. **68** Igitur quidam monachus uita et opinione perfectus habitans in deserto terre Sennaar, nomine Barlaam, hec que circa filium regis agebantur per spiritum cognouit et mercatoris habitum sumens ad ciuitatem illam deuenit. **69** Accedensque pedagogo filii regis locutus est dicens: **70** "Ego, cum negotiator sim, lapidem pretiosum uenalem habeo, qui cecis lumen tribuit, surdis aures aperit, mutos loqui facit, insipientibus sapientiam infundit. **71** Nunc igitur duc me ad filium regis ut hunc sibi tradam."
72 Cui ille: "Videris homo mature prudentie, sed uerba tua prudentie non concordant. **73** Verumtamen cum lapidum notitiam habeam, ipsum lapidem mihi ostende et, si talis ut asseris fuerit comprobatus, a filio regis honores maximos consequeris."
74 Ad quem ille: "Lapis meus hanc insuper habet uirtutem, quia qui non habet sanam oculorum aciem et qui non seruat integram castitatem, si forte illum aspexerit, ipsam uirtutem quam habet uisibilem perdit. **75** Ego autem medicinalis artis non expers uideo te sanos oculos non habere, filium autem regis audiui pudicum esse et oculos pulcherrimos et sanos habere." **76** Cui ille: "Si sic est, noli mihi ostendere, quia et oculos sanos non habeo et in peccatis sordesco."

5.1. BARLAAM'S FIRST PARABLE: THE HERALD OF DEATH AND THE FOUR CHESTS

77 Nuntians igitur hoc filio regis ipsum ad eum quantocius introduxit. **78** Cum ergo introductus fuisset et rex eum reuerenter suscepisset, ait Barlaam: **79** "Hoc, rex, bene fecisti, quia de foris paruitati apparenti non attendisti: **80** nam rex quidam magnus in curru deaurato procedens, cum quibusdam attritas uestes indutis et macie attenuatis obuiasset, continuo de curru exiliens ad eius pedes procidens ipsos adorauit et surgens in oscula eius ruit. **81** Proceres autem eius indigne hoc ferentes, sed regem super hoc arguere formidantes, fratri retulerunt quomodo rex magnificentie regali indigna fecisset, frater autem regem super hoc redarguit. **82** Erat autem regi consuetudo quod, quando aliquis morti tradendus erat, rex ante eius ianuam preconem cum tuba ad hoc deputata mittebat. **83** Vespere igitur ueniente ante fratris ianuam tubam sonari fecit. **84** Quod ille audiens et de sua salute desperans totam noctem insomnem duxit et testamentum fecit, mane autem facto indutus nigris

uestibus cum uxore et filiis ad fores palatii lugens accessit. **85** Quem rex
ad se ingredi faciens dixit: **86** "O stulte, si preconem fratris tui, cui nihil
te deliquisse cognoscis, adeo timuisti, quomodo precones domini mei, in
quem adeo peccaui, timere non debeam, qui sonabilius mihi tuba mortem
significant et terribilem iudicis aduentum denuntiant?" **87** Deinde
quatuor capsas fieri iussit et duas earum extrinsecus auro undique operiri
et ossibus mortuorum putridis impleri, duas uero pice liniri et gemmis
et margaritis pretiosis impleri fecit. **88** Vocansque illos magnates quos
sciebat querimoniam apud fratrem deposuisse, quatuor illas capsas ante
eos posuit et que pretiosiores essent inquisiuit. **89** Illi uero duas deauratas
magni esse pretii, reliquas uero uilis pretii esse indicauerunt. **90** Precepit
igitur rex deauratas aperiri et continuo inde fetor intolerabilis exhalauit.
91 Quibus rex: "Hec illis similes sunt, qui gloriosis uestibus sunt amicti,
intus uero immunditia uitiorum pleni." **92** Deinde alias aperiri fecit et ecce
odor inde mirabilis exhalauit. **93** Quibus rex: "Iste illis pauperrimis quos
honoraui similes sunt qui, etsi uilibus uestimentis operiantur, intus tamen
omni uirtutum odore resplendent; **94** uos autem solum que de foris sunt
attenditis et que deintus sunt non consideratis." **95** Secundum igitur illum
regem tu quoque fecisti bene suscipiens me."

5.2. BARLAAM'S SECOND PARABLE: THE ARCHER
AND THE NIGHTINGALE

96 Incipiens igitur Barlaam cepit ei de mundi creatione et hominis
preuaricatione ac filii dei incarnatione, passione et resurrectione longum
sermonem retexere necnon et de die iudicii et retributione bonorum et
malorum multa ponere et seruientes ydolis plurimum exprobrare ac de eorum
fatuitate tale exemplum proferre dicens: **97** "Sagittarius quidam auiculam
paruam nomine philomenam capiens, cum uellet eam occidere, uox data est
philomene et ait: **98** "Quid tibi proderit, o homo, si me occideris? **99** Neque
enim uentrem tuum de me implere ualebis, sed, si me dimittere uelles, tria
tibi mandata darem, que, si diligentius conseruares, magnam inde utilitatem
consequi posses." **100** Ille uero ad eius loquelam stupefactus promisit quod
eam dimitteret si hec sibi mandata proferret. **101** Et illa: "Numquam rem
que apprehendi non potest apprehendere studeas; **102** de re perdita et
irrecuperabili nunquam doleas; **103** uerbum incredibile nunquam credas.
104 Hec tria custodi et bene tibi erit." **105** Ille autem, ut promiserat, eam
dimisit, philomena igitur per aera uolitans dixit ei: **106** "Ve tibi, homo, quam
malum consilium habuisti et quam magnum thesaurum hodie perdidisti!
107 Est enim in meis uisceribus margarita que struthionis ouum sua uincit
magnitudine." **108** Quod ille audiens ualde contristatus est quod eam

dimiserit et eam apprehendere conabatur dicens: **109** "Veni in domum meam et omnem tibi humanitatem exhibebo et honorifice te dimittam." **110** Cui philomena: "Nunc pro certo cognoui te fatuum esse. **111** Nam ex hiis que tibi dixi nullum profectum habuisti, quia et de me perdita et irrecuperabili doles et me temptasti capere, cum nequeas meo itinere pergere, et insuper margaritam tam grandem in meis uisceribus esse credidisti, cum ego tota ad magnitudinem oui struthionis non ualeam pertingere." **112** Sic ergo stulti sunt illi qui confidunt in ydolis quia plasmatos a se adorant et custoditos a se custodes suos appellant."

5.3. BARLAAM'S THIRD PARABLE: THE MAN IN THE WELL

113 Cepitque contra fallacem mundi delectationem et uanitatem multa disputare et plura ad hoc exempla adducere dicens: **114** "Qui delectationes corporales desiderant et animas suas fame mori permittunt, similes sunt cuidam homini qui, dum a facie unicornis ne ab eo deuoraretur uelocius fugeret, in quodam baratrum magnum cecidit. **115** Dum autem caderet, manibus arbustulam quandam apprehendit et in base quadam lubrica et instabili pedes fixit. **116** Respiciens uero uidit duos mures, unum album et alium nigrum, incessanter radicem arbustule quam apprehenderat corrodentes et iam prope erat ut ipsam absciderent. **117** In fundo autem baratri uidit draconem terribilem spirantem ignem et aperto ore ipsum deuorare cupientem, super basem uero, ubi pedes tenebat, uidit quatuor aspidum capita inde prodeuntia. **118** Eleuans autem oculos uidit exiguum mellis de ramis illius arbustule oblitusque periculi in quo undique positus erat, se ipsum dulcedini illius modici mellis totum dedit. **119** Vnicornis autem mortis tenet figuram que hominem semper persequitur et apprehendere cupit, baratrum uero mundus est omnibus malis plenus. **120** Arbustula uniuscuiusque uita est que per horas diei et noctis quasi per murem album et nigrum incessanter consumitur et incisioni appropinquat. **121** Basis quatuor aspidum corpus ex quatuor elementis compositum, quibus inordinatis corporis compago dissoluitur. **122** Draco terribilis os inferni cunctos deuorare cupiens, dulcedo ramusculi delectatio fallax mundi, per quam homo seducitur ut periculum suum minime intueatur."

5.4. BARLAAM'S FOURTH PARABLE: THE MAN AND HIS THREE FRIENDS

123 Addidit quoque dicens: **124** "Similes sunt iterum mundi amatores homini qui tres amicos habuit. **125** Quorum unum plus quam se, secundum tantum quantum se, tertium minus quam se et quasi nihil dilexit. **126** In magno

itaque periculo positus et a rege citatus cucurrit ad primum amicum eius
auxilium querens et qualiter eum semper dilexerit commemorans.
127 Cui ille: "Nescio quis sis, o homo, habeo alios amicos cum quibus me
hodie letari oportet quos et amicos amodo possidebo. **128** Prebeo tamen
tibi duo ciliciola ut habeas quibus ualeas operiri."**129** Confusus igitur ad
secundum abiit et similiter eius auxilium postulauit. **130** Cui ille: "Non uacat
mihi tecum subire agonem; **131** curis etenim multis circumdor, modicum
tamen usque ad ostium palatii te sociabo et statim domum reuertar propriis
uacans negotiis." **132** Tristis igitur et desperans ad tertium amicum perrexit
sibique facie dimissa dixit: **133** "Non habeo os loquendi ad te quoniam ut
debui non amaui te, sed in tribulatione circumdatus et ab amicis destitutus
rogo ut mihi auxilium feras et mihi ueniam prebeas."**134** Et ille hylari uultu
dixit: **135** "Certe amicum carissimum fateor te esse et tui licet modici beneficii
non immemor precedam te et apud regem interueniam pro te ne in manibus
inimicorum tradet te." **136** Primus igitur amicus est diuitiarum possessio pro
quibus homo multis periculis subiacet, ueniente uero mortis termino nihil
ex hiis omnibus nisi uiles accepit ad sepeliendum panniculos. **137** Secundus
amicus est uxor, filii et parentes qui tantum usque ad monumentum secum
pergentes, protinus reuertuntur suis uacantes curis. **138** Tertius amicus
est fides, spes et caritas et elemosina et cetera bona opera que nos, cum de
corpore eximus, possunt precedere et pro nobis apud deum interuenire et ab
inimicis demonibus nos liberare."

5.5. BARLAAM'S FIFTH PARABLE: THE KING FOR ONE YEAR

139 Hoc insuper addidit dicens: **140** "In quadam magna ciuitate consuetudo
fuit quod hominem extraneum et ignotum omni anno in principem eligebant
cui omni potestate accepta quidquid uolebat facere licitum erat et sine omni
constitutione terram regebat. **141** Illo igitur in omnibus deliciis permanente et
semper sibi sic esse existimante, repente ciues in eum insurgebant et per totam
ciuitatem nudum trahentes in remotam insulam exulem transmittebant, ubi
nec cibum nec uestimentum inueniens fame et frigore urgebatur. **142** Tandem
quidam alius sublimatus in regno cum illorum ciuium consuetudinem
didicisset, infinitos thesauros ad insulam illam premisit, ubi post annum in
exilium relegatus ceteris fame deficientibus ille immensis deliciis abundabat.
143 Ciuitas hec mundus iste est; **144** ciues tenebrarum principes qui nos
falsa mundi delectatione illiciunt, nobisque insperantibus mors superuenit et
in locum tenebrarum demergimur; **145** diuitiarum uero ad eternum locum
premissio fit manibus egenorum."

5.6. BARLAAM'S SIXTH PARABLE: THE RICH YOUTH AND THE POOR MAIDEN

Josaphat Receives Baptism

146 Igitur cum Barlaam perfecte filium regis docuisset et ipse eum iam relicto patre sequi uellet, dixit ad eum Barlaam: **147** "Si hoc feceris, cuidam iuueni similis eris qui, cum quandam nobilem nollet desponsare uxorem, ipse renuens aufugit et in quendam locum deueniens uirginem quandam, cuiusdam senis pauperis filiam, laborantem et ore deum laudantem uidit. **148** Ad quam ille: "Quid est quod agis, mulier? **149** Cum enim ita pauper sis, gratiam tamen agis deo ac si magna recepisses ab eo." **150** Ad quem illa: "Sicut parua medicina sepe a magno languore liberat, sic gratiarum actio in paruis donis magnorum efficitur auctrix donorum. **151** Hec tamen que extrinsecus sunt nostra non sunt, sed ea que in nobis sunt et nostra sunt a deo magna accepi quia me ad suam ymaginem fecit, intellectum mihi dedit, ad suam me gloriam uocauit et ianuam regni sui iam mihi aperuit; **152** pro tantis ergo et tam magnis donis ipsum laudare conueni." **153** Videns iuuenis eius prudentiam eam a patre suo in uxorem petiit. **154** Cui ille: "Filiam meam accipere non uales quia diuitum et nobilium filius es, ego autem pauper sum." **155** Sed cum illo omnino instaret, ait senex: **156** "Non possum eam tibi dare ut in domum patris tui ducas eam, cum unica mihi sit." **157** Et ille: "Apud uos manebo et uobis me in omnibus conformabo." **158** Deponens igitur pretiosum ornamentum habitum senis induit et apud eum manens ipsam in uxorem accepit. **159** Postquam uero senex diutius eum probauit, in thalamum eum duxit et immensum pondus diuitiarum, quantum nunquam uiderat, sibi ostendit et omnia sibi dedit."

160 Dixit autem Iosaphat: **161** "Conuenienter me ista tangit narratio et a te hoc dictum esse de me existimo, sed dic mihi, pater, quot annorum es et ubi conuersaris, quia a te nunquam uolo separari." **162** Et ille: "Annorum sum XLV in desertis terre Sennaar degens."

163 Ad quem Iosaphat: "Amplius mihi pater appares LXX annorum."

164 Et ille: "Si a natiuitate mea omnes annos meos queris discere, bene eos existimasti, sed nullo modo a me in mensura uite computantur quotquot in uanitate mundi expensi sunt; **165** tunc enim in interiori homine mortuus eram et annos mortis nunquam uite nominabo." **166** Cum igitur Iosaphat eum in desertum sequi uellet dixit Barlaam: **167** "Si hoc feceris et tuo consortio carebo et persecutionis fratribus meis auctor existam, sed cum oportunum tempus uideris, ad me uenies." **168** Barlaam igitur filium regis baptizans et in fide optime instruens eum osculatus est et ad locum suum reuersus est.

Part 6: King Avenir's Effort to Bring the Prince Back to Idol-Worship with the Help of Fake Barlaam

169 Postquam autem rex filium christianum factum audiuit, in dolore nimio positus est. **170** Quem quidam amicus suus nomine Arachis consolans ait: **171** "Cognosco, rex senem quendam heremitam, qui de nostra secta est, qui per omnia Barlaam similis est; **172** hic igitur Barlaam se simulans primo christianorum fidem defendet, deinde se superari permittet et omnia que docuerat reuocabit et sic filius regis ad nos redibit." **173** Assumpto igitur predicto principe magno exercitu ad querendum Barlaam iuit et heremitam illum capiens se Barlaam cepisse dixit. **174** Quod filius regis audiens, captum scilicet magistrum amare fleuit, sed postmodum per dei reuelationem hunc non esse cognouit. **175** Ingressus igitur pater ad filium ait: **176** "Fili mi, in tristitia magna me posuisti et meam canitiem inhonorasti et lumen oculorum meorum abstulisti; **177** quare, fili, hoc fecisti et deorum meorum cultum reliquisti?" **178** Cui ille: "Tenebras, pater, fugi, ad lumen cucurri, errorem deserui et ueritatem agnoui, noli autem frustra laborare, quoniam nunquam a Christo me posses reuocare, sicut enim tibi impossibile est altitudinem celi manu tangere aut maximum siccare pelagus, sic et istud esse cognosce." **179** Tunc rex ait: **180** "Et quis horum mihi est auctor malorum, nisi ego, qui tam magnifica tibi feci, que nunquam aliquis patrum fecit filio suo? **181** Quapropter prauitas tue uoluntatis et contentio effrenata aduersus caput meum te insanire fecit. **182** Merito astrologi in natiuitate tua dixerunt te arrogantem et parentibus inobedientem futurum. **183** Nunc uero nisi mihi acquieueris a mea discedes filiatione et pro patre inimicus effectus illa tibi faciam que nec hostibus adhuc feci." **184** Cui Iosaphat: "Cur, rex, tristaris quia bonorum particeps sum effectus? **185** Quis unquam pater in filii sui prosperitate tristis apparuit? **186** Non ergo iam patrem uocabo te sed, si mihi aduersaberis, sicut a serpente fugiam a te." **187** Rex igitur ab eo cum ira discedens Arachi amico notam fecit filii duritiam. **188** Qui sibi consuluit ut non asperis uerbis cum eo uteretur, quia blandis et lenibus puer melius traheretur. **189** Sequenti igitur die rex ad filium uenit et circumplectens osculabatur eum dicens: **190** "Fili dulcissime, honora canitiem patris tui, uerere, fili, patrem tuum; **191** an nescis quale bonum est patri obedire et eum letificare, sicut e contra malum est ipsos exacerbare? **192** Quotquot enim fecerunt, male perierunt."

Part 7: The Debate between Fake Barlaam (Nachor) and the Pagan Orators

193 Cui Iosaphat: "Tempus amandi et tempus odiendi, tempus pacis et tempus belli; **194** nullo enim modo auertentibus nos a deo obedire debemus, siue sit pater, siue sit mater." **195** Videns igitur pater eius constantiam ait: **196** "Ex quo tuam uideo pertinaciam nec mihi obedire uis, saltem ueni et ambo pariter ueritati credamus. **197** Barlaam enim, qui te seduxit a me uinctus tenetur; **198** nostri igitur et uestri cum Barlaam conueniant et preconem mittam ut omnes Galilei sine timore ueniant, et disputatione incepta, si uester Barlaam obtinuerit, uobis credemus; **199** si autem nostri, nobis consentietis." **200** Quod cum regis filio placuisset et illi cum simulato Barlaam ordinassent quomodo prius debebat simulare se fidem christianorum defendere et postea se promittere superari, omnes insimul conuenerunt. **201** Conuersus igitur Iosaphat ad Nachor dixit: **202** "Nosti, o Barlaam, qualiter me docuisti. **203** Si igitur fidem quam me docuisti defenderis, in doctrina tua usque ad finem uite permanebo. **204** Si autem superatus fueris, statim in te meam contumeliam uindicabo et cor tuum et linguam manibus extrahens canibus dabo ne alii amplius presumant filios regum in errorem mittere." **205** Hiis auditis Nachor tristis et pauidus uehementer effectus est, uidens se ipsum in foueam quam fecit decidisse et laqueo suo comprehensum esse. **206** Animaduertens igitur cognouit melius esse filio regis adherere ut periculum mortis euadere posset. **207** Rex autem sibi palam dixerat ut fidem suam sine timore defenderet. **208** Vnus ergo rethorum surgens dixit: **209** "Tu es Barlaam qui filium regis seduxisti?" **210** Et ille: "Ego sum Barlaam qui filium regis non in errorem misi, sed ab errore liberaui." **211** Et rethor: "Cum eximii et mirabiles uiri deos nostros adorauerunt, quomodo tu aduersus eos audes insurgere?" **212** Et ille respondens ait: **213** "Chaldei, Greci et Egyptii errantes creaturas deos esse dixerunt. **214** Nam Chaldei elementa deos arbitrati sunt, cum creata sint ad utilitatem hominum ut eorum dominationi subiaceant et multis passionibus corrumpantur. **215** Greci quoque nefandos homines deos esse putant, sicut Saturnum, quem aiunt filios suos comedisse et uirilia sibi abscidisse et in mare proiecisse et Venerem inde natam fuisse, a filio quoque suo Ioue alligatum et in tartarum proiectum esse. **216** Iupiter quoque rex aliorum deorum esse describitur quem tamen in animalia sepe transformatum dicunt ut adulteria committeret. **217** Venerem quoque deam adulteram esse dicunt, nam aliquando habuit mechum Martem, aliquando Adonidem. **218** Egyptii autem animalia coluerunt scilicet ouem, uitulum, porcum et huiusmodi. **219** Christiani autem filium altissimi colunt qui de celo descendit et carnem assumpsit." **220** Cepit igitur Nachor fidem christianorum euidenter defendere et rationibus communire, ita quod rethores illi muti effecti nihil omnino respondere sciuerunt. **221** Iosaphat igitur uehementer exultabat, eo quod dominus per inimicum ueritatis ueritatem defendisset, rex autem furore nimio repletus est. **222** Iussit igitur consilium dissolui quasi de hiis sequenti die denuo tractaturus, dixitque Iosaphat patri: **223** "Aut magistrum meum permitte mecum hac nocte manere ut simul de responsionibus fiendis crastino conferamus et tu tuos tecum assumas et cum eis conferas aut tuis mecum permissis accipe meum. **224** Alioquin non iustitiam sed uiolentiam exercebis". **225** Quapropter Nachor sibi concessit spem adhuc habens quod eum seduceret. **226** Cum igitur filius regis cum Nachor domum redisset, dixit ei Iosaphat: **227** "Ne putes me ignorare quis sis; **228** scio te non esse Barlaam, sed Nachor astrologum." **229** Incipiensque Iosaphat uiam salutis ei predicauit et ad fidem conuertens mane ad heremum misit ubi baptismum suscipiens heremiticam uitam duxit.

Part 8: *The Prince in the Cave Allegory and Josaphat's Sexual Temptations*

230 Magus autem quidam nomine Theodas hec que gerebantur audiens ad regem uenit et quod filium suum ad leges patrias redire faceret promisit. **231** Cui rex: "Si hoc feceris statuam auream tibi erigam et ipsi sicut diis sacrificium offeram." **232** Et ille: "A filio tuo cunctos remoue et mulieres decoras et ornatas introduci precipe ut semper cum eo sint et ministrent ei et conuersentur et morentur cum eo. **233** Ego autem unum de spiritibus meis ad eum dirigam qui eum ad libidinem inflammabit. **234** Nihil enim iuuenes sic potest seducere sicut facies mulierum. **235** Rex enim quidam cum filium uix habuisset dixerunt peritissimi medici quod si infra annos decem solem uel lunam uiderit lumine oculorum priuabitur. **236** Rex igitur in quadam petra spelunca excisa filium ibi usque ad annos decem manere fecit. **237** Quibus finitis iussit rex ut omnium rerum genera ante eum adducerentur ut omnium nomina et notitiam posset habere. **238** Adductis igitur ante eum auro et argento, lapidibus pretiosis, uestibus splendidis, equis regalibus et omnium rerum generibus, cum de uniuscuiusque rei nomine interrogaret, ministri omnium sibi nomina indicabant.

239 Cum autem nomen mulierum discere anxie quereret, spatharius regis ludendo dixit demones eas esse que homines seducunt. **240** Rege igitur interrogante filium quid de omnibus que uiderat plus amaret: **241** "Quid," inquit, "pater, aliud nisi demones illos qui seducunt homines? **242** In nullo enim sicut in hiis sic exarsit anima mea." **243** Non igitur aliter putes te filium tuum superare nisi hoc modo." **244** Rex igitur omnibus ministris eiectis

puellas decoras ei sociauit que eum semper ad libidinem prouocabant nec
habebat alium ad quem respiceret aut cum quo loqueretur uel cum quo
uesceretur. **245** Malignus uero spiritus a mago missus in iuuenem irruit et
magnum intus caminum ignis accendit. **246** Malignus igitur spiritus intus
inflammabat, puelle autem exterius dirum excitabant ardorem. **247** Qui
se tam fortiter uexari sentiens turbabatur et deo se totum recommendans
diuinam consolationem recepit et omnis temptatio abscessit. **248** Deinde
quandam puellam pulcherrimam cuiusdam regis filiam, sed patre orbatam
ad eum misit. **249** Cui cum uir dei predicaret illa respondit: **250** "Si me ab
ydolorum cultura saluare desideras coniungere mihi nuptiarum copula.
251 Nam et christiani coniugia non abhorrent, sed laudant, quia patriarche
eorum et prophete et Petrus eorum apostolus coniuges habuerunt." **252** Ad
quam ille: "Inaniter, mulier, ista mihi prosequeris. **253** Permittitur quidem
christianis uxores ducere, sed non hiis qui promiserunt Christo uirginitatem
seruare." **254** Et illa: "Sit ita ut uis; **255** sed, si animam meam saluare
desideras, unam minimam petitionem mihi perfice, concumbe mecum
tantum hac nocte et promitto tibi quod summo diluculo efficiar christiana.
256 Nam si, ut dicitis, gaudium est angelis in celo super uno peccatore
penitentiam agente, auctori conuersionis nonne magna merces debetur?
257 Semel tantum mihi acquiesce et sic me ipsam saluabis." **258** Illa igitur
turrim anime illius fortiter commouere cepit. **259** Quod demon uidens sociis
suis ait: **260** "Videtis quomodo puella ista concussit que nos non potuimus
concutere. **261** Venite ergo et in eum fortiter irruamus ex quo congruum
tempus inuenimus."

Part 9: Josaphat's Divine Dream and King Avenir's Conversion

262 Cernens igitur sanctus iuuenis se tam fortiter captiuatum quia et
concupiscentia incitabat et salus unius puelle, dyabolo suggerente, ipsum
commouebat, lacrimis infusus orationi se dedit. **263** In qua oratione
obdormiens uidit se duci in quoddam pratum decoris floribus exornatum ubi
folia arborum dulcem sonum reddebant, aura quadam grata agitata et odor
mirificus emanabat, ubi fructus uisu speciosissimi et gustu desiderabiles, ubi
sedes posite erant auro et gemmis fabricate, lecti lucidi cum pretiosissimis
ornamentis, aque limpidissime preterfluentes. **264** Dehinc in ciuitatem
ipsum introduxerunt, cuius muri ex auro obrizo erant quod claritate
mirabili refulgebat, ubi etherei quidam exercitus canticum cantantes quod
auris mortalium non audiuit, dictumque est: **265** "Iste est locus beatorum."
266 Cum autem uiri uellent eum reducere, rogabat ut ibi eum manere
permitterent. **267** Qui dixerunt: **268** "Cum labore multo adhuc uenies huc, si

tamen tibi uim inferre poteris." **269** Deinde ad loca teterrima ipsum duxerunt omni feditate plena dictumque est: **270** "Iste est locus iniustorum." **271** Cum autem euigilasset pulchritudo illius puelle et ceterarum stercore feditior ei uidebatur. **272** Verum cum maligni spiritus ad Theodam redissent et ipse eos exprobraret, dixerunt: **273** "Priusquam signo crucis signaretur, super ipsum irruentes fortiter ipsum conturbauimus; **274** ut autem se signo crucis muniuit, nos persecutus est cum ira." **275** Tunc Theodas cum rege ad eum intrauit sperans quod ei persuadere posset, sed predictus magus captus est ab eo quem capere uoluit et ab eo conuersus baptisma suscepit et laudabilem uitam duxit. **276** Rex igitur desperans dimisit ei de consilio amicorum medium regni sui. **277** Ille autem licet desertum tota mente desideraret, tamen propter fidei dilatationem ad tempus ipsum regnum suscepit ac in suis ciuitatibus templa et cruces erexit et omnes ad Christum conuertit.

Part 10: Josaphat Becomes Saint

278 Pater autem tandem filii rationibus et predicationibus assensum prebens, fidem Christi recepit et baptismum suscipiens et totum regnum filio dimittens ipse penitentie operibus uacabat et post hoc laudabiliter uitam finiuit. **279** Iosaphat autem Barachiam regem pronuntians pluries fugere uoluit, sed semper a populo captus uix tandem ualuit. **280** Cum igitur per desertum pergeret, cuidam pauperi regalem habitum dedit et ipse in pauperrima ueste remansit. **281** Dyabolus autem multas ei parabat insidias; **282** aliquando enim gladio euaginato in eum irruebat et percutere minabatur nisi desisteret, aliquando in forma ferarum apparebat frendens et dirum mugitum emittens. **283** Ille autem dicebat: **284** "Dominus mihi adiutor est. **285** Non timebo quid faciat mihi homo." **286** Duobus igitur annis in heremo Iosaphat uagabundus mansit nec Barlaam inuenire potuit, tandem speluncam inuenit et ante ostium stans dicebat: **287** "Benedic, pater, benedic!" **288** Cuius uocem Barlaam audiens foras exiliit et osculantes se feruentissimis sese alterutrum amplexibus constringebant nec satiari poterant. **289** Retulit autem Iosaphat Barlaam omnia que acciderant et ille immensas gratias egit deo. **290** Mansit autem Iosaphat ibidem annis multis in abstinentia mirabili et uirtute, tandem completis diebus Barlaam in pace quieuit circa annos domini CCCLXXX. **291** Iosaphat igitur in anno XXV regnum deserens triginta quinque annis heremiticum laborem subiit et sic multis clarus uirtutibus in pace quieuit et cum corpore Barlaam positus fuit. **292** Quod audiens rex Barachias illuc cum multo exercitu uenit et corpora reuerenter assumens in ciuitatem suam transtulit, ad quorum tumulum miracula multa fiunt.

Commentary

Text with Classical Latin Orthography, Commentary, and Vocabulary

NOTE: In this version of the text, Medieval Latin spellings are changed according to the Classical Latin norms. <u>The words with normalized spelling are underlined</u>.

Introduction and summary of the legend. This Latin version is translated from the Greek text of John of Damascus and tells the story of Barlaam who converted King Avenir's son, Prince Josaphat, to Christianity. King Avenir persecutes Christians.

1 Barlaam, cuius <u>historiam</u> Iohannes Damascenus diligenti studio compilauit, operante in eo diuina gratia sanctum Iosaphat regem ad fidem conuertit.
2 Etenim cum uniuersa India christianis et monachis plena esset, surrexit rex quidam <u>praepotens</u> nomine Auenir qui christianos et <u>praecipue</u> monachos plurimum persequebatur.

1 *Iohannes Damascenus* = The Syrian-born saint and theologian of the 8th century John of Damascus, one of the Fathers of the Eastern Orthodox Church, was believed until the 19th century to be the author of the legend. Neither Jacobus nor the translators of the Greek and Latin versions knew of the Indian origin of the legend. John died in 749, about two hundred and fifty years before the tale was translated into Greek (11th century) and therefore could not have authored or even translated it.[1] About two hundred years after Jacobus, a 15th-century reader of the Venetian traveller and writer Marco Polo (1254–1324) noticed the similarities between Marco Polo's description of the life of Sagamoni Borcan (the Buddha) and the story of Barlaam and Josaphat,[2] well known to his readers through summaries of the legend like the one that we are reading here (cf. Introd. 1.1).

---

1. Cf. Lopez and McCracken (2014) 130.
2. Lopez and McCracken (2014) 10; 172.

diligenti: ablative singular, comes from the **1-ending third declension adjective** *diligens, diligentis*. Datives and ablatives both end with an *-i* in **third declension adjectives**.

operante . . . gratia: **ablative absolute**, "with divine grace working within him." *sanctum Iosaphat regem* is the DO of *conuertit*. Because the proper name *Iosaphat* is indeclinable, its accusative case can be guessed from its adjective *sanctum* and from *regem*, which is its noun in apposition (A&G 282). Throughout the legend, the title *rex* is given to King Avenir, not to Josaphat. The introduction anticipates the end of the story where Josaphat will become a king and will renounce his earthly kingdom to become a saint.

2 *universa India*: according to legend, entire India was converted to Christianity by Saint Thomas (the one known as Doubting Thomas). Marco Polo in the 14th century wrote about his visit to Saint Thomas's tomb in India.[3] The events that we are reading are assumed to have taken place after India's relapse into idol-worship and paganism some time after Thomas's ministry, described in the Greek version of the legend[4] (cf. Introd. 3.2).

rex quidam <u>praepotens</u> nomine Auenir: this noun phrase is the subject of *surrexit*. Verbs often precede their **subjects** in this text (cf. G. 6.2).

nomine Auenir: *Auenir* is noun in apposition (A&G 282) to *rex* and *nomine* is **ablative of specification (respect)**, i.e. "Auenir by name."

1 *diligens, diligentis (adj.)* diligent
compilo, -are, -aui, -atum compile (LL)
gratia, ae, f. grace (LL)
Iosaphat (indeclinable proper name) Josaphat, the main protagonist in the
    legend
fides, ei, f. faith, Christian faith (LL); trust (CL)
2 *etenim (conj)* and indeed, as a matter of fact
monachus, i, m. monk
plenus, -a, -um full of (+ abl)
surgo, -ere, -rexi, -rectum rule, rise to power
praepotens, ntis (adj.) very powerful
praecipue (adv.) especially
plurimum (adv.) very much
persequor, -sequi, -secutus sum persecute

---

3. Cf. Lopez and McCracken (2014) 124–25.
4. Woodward and Mattingly (1997) 9.

Part 1: *King Avenir Encounters Christianity at His Own Court*

King Avenir's friend, an anonymous noble at his court joins a monastic order.
The king is angry because of that.

3 Accidit autem ut quidam regis amicus et in palatio suo primus diuina
commotus gratia regiam aulam relinqueret et monasticum ordinem introiret.
4 Quod rex audiens et <u>prae</u> ira insaniens eum per <u>quaeque</u> deserta inquiri
fecit et uix inuentum ad se adduci mandauit.

3 *in palatio suo* = CL *in palatio eius: suo* refers to the king ("in his, the king's
palace"). For the LL use of *suus* referring to someone other than the subject
cf. G. 4.1. The word *palatium* originates from the Palatine Hill in Rome where
most of the imperial palaces were located.
4 *quod rex audiens: quod* functions as **connecting relative** pronoun ("the king,
hearing this").
prae ira: the preposition has a causal meaning ("because of anger").
4 *eum . . . inquiri*: LL infinitive for result clause with *fecit* = *iussit* (cf. G. 3.1).
quaeque: from *quisque, quaeque, quodque* (each, every), neuter plural pronoun
with *deserta* ("all desert places").

3 *palatium, ii, n.* palace
primus, i, m. (substantive) nobleman
commoueo, -ere, -moui, -motum move, stir up
regius, -a, -um (adj.) royal, regal
aula, ae, f. hall
ordo, ordinis, f. order, rank
introeo, -ire, -iui, -itum enter
4 *ira, ae, f.* wrath, rage
insanio, -ire, -iui, -itum be mad
quisque, quaeque, quidque each, every
deserta, orum, n. (pl.) desert places (LL)
inquiro, -ere, -quisivi, -quisitum seek out, investigate
uix (adv.) with difficulty
inuenio, -ire, -ueni, -uentum find
mando, -are, -aui, -atum order (LL)

King Avenir and the Christian noble set rules of engagement for their debate
about matters of faith.

5 Vidensque eum uili tunica coopertum et fame maceratum, qui splendidis
uestimentis ornabatur et multis deliciis affluere consueuerat, dixit ei:
6 "O stulte ac mentis perdite, cur honorem in contumeliam commutasti
et te ludum puerorum fecisti?" **7** Cui ille: "Si huius a me rationem audire
desideras inimicos tuos a te procul abicias." **8** Rege autem qui essent huius
inimici <u>quaerente</u>, ait: **9** "Ira et concupiscentia. <u>Haec</u> enim impediunt ne
ueritas uideatur. **10** Assideant autem ad audentiam dicendorum prudentia et
<u>aequitas.</u>" **11** Cui rex: "Fiat ut loqueris."

6 *mentis perdite:* the genitive of specification (A&G 349d) *mentis* describes
in what respect the person is debilitated. *Perdite* is the **vocative** of the
substantively used perfect passive participle of *perdo.* The phrase is a
colloquial expression of insult ("you, who have been debilitated in respect to
your mind" or "you, who have lost your mind").
fecisti forms a **factitive sentence pattern** here.
7 *abicias:* **jussive subjunctive** expressing polite command.
8 *Rege . . . quaerente:* **ablative absolute** with embedded **indirect question.** CL
very rarely embeds clauses inside **ablative absolutes** (cf. G. 6.1).
10 *ad audentiam dicendorum:* read *audentiam* as *audientiam.*[5] *Dicendorum*
is genitive neuter plural **gerundive**, a LL construction (for the LL **gerundive**
without the connotation of necessity or obligation, cf. G. 2.5.) The substantive
use of the neuter plural **gerundive** is very rare in CL and even then, it occurs
only in the nominative and accusative case.[6] Translate "at the hearing of the
things about to be said."
11 *loqueris = loquaris* in **noun-result clause** (cf. G. 8 on ungrammatical Latin).

5 *uilis, -e (adj.)* common, worthless
cooperio, -ire, -operui, -opertum cover up completely
fames, famis, f. famine, hunger
macero, -are, -aui, -atum weaken
uestimentum, i, n. garment
orno, -are, -aui, -atum equip, dressed
deliciae, arum, f. (pl.) delights, pleasure
affluo, -ere, -fluxi, -fluxus flow towards; abound
consuesco, -ere, -sueui, -suetum be accustomed to
6 *stultus, i, m.* fool
perdo, -ere, -didi, -ditum ruin, debilitate
contumelia, ae, f. disgrace, insult

---

5. Jacobus's manuscripts contain an error here. The long Latin version (*Vulgata*) has *audientiam*
(cf. Cruz Palma (2001) chapter 11, p. 116.

6. Examples can be found in Catullus, Horace, Ovid, and Livy, e.g., *fanda, nefanda, dicenda,
tacenda.* Cf. Hofmann-Szantyr (1972) 371, 202A.

commuto, -are, -aui, -atum change
ludus, i, m. game, entertainment
7 *ratio, onis, f.* reason
desidero, -are, -aui, -atum desire, want
procul (adv.) far away
abicio, -icere, -ieci, -iectum throw away
ait (irregular verb 3rd pers. sg) he says
9 *concupiscentia, ae, f.* desire
impedio, -ire, -iui, -itum hinder
10 *assideo, -ere, -sedi, -sessum* preside
audentia = audientia, ae, f. hearing (LL)
aequitas, tatis, f. equity, fairness

The philosophy of King Avenir's former friend, now a Christian monk and his reason for adopting the monastic way of life.

12 Et ille: "Insipientes ea quae sunt despiciunt quasi non sint; **13** quae uero non sunt quasi sint apprehendere moliuntur. **14** Qui autem non gustauerit eorum quae sunt dulcedinem, non poterit eorum quae non sunt addiscere ueritatem." **15** Multa autem illo de mysterio incarnationis et fidei prosequente, rex ait: **16** "Nisi tibi in principio promisissem quod de medio concilii iram remouerem, nunc utique igni tuas carnes traderem. **17** Surge igitur et fuge ex oculis meis ne ultra te uideam et male te perdam." **18** Vir autem dei tristis abscessit eo quod martyrium perpessus non esset.

12–13 *ea quae sunt* (Greek *ta onta*): "the things that exist" or "the things that are real" is a philosophical term that refers to unchanging realities that are transcendental and invisible to the physical eyes. "The things that do not truly exist" (*quae uero non sunt*), mentioned later, refers to impermanent, changing things that do not truly exist in the sense that they are in a process of constant flux and transformation. In this view, the world that we see around us has no reality or true existence (*quae uero non sunt*). The longer Latin version explains:

> *Existentia quidem uocauit sermo aeterna et non mutabilia, non existentia uero praesentem uitam et delicias atque fallacem prosperitatem . . .*[7]

> "The discourse has called real (existent) the things that are eternal and unchanging while it has called unreal (non-existent) the present life, its delights and deceptive prosperity. . . ."

---

7. In the original LL orthography: *Existencia quidem uocauit sermo eterna et non mutabilia, non existencia uero presentem uitam et delicias atque fallacem prosperitatem . . .* (Cruz-Palma (2001) 118, chapter 12).

For the place of this chapter in the larger context of the legend, see Introd. 2.3.
quasi + subjunctive means "as (would be the case) if/ as though." The idea is
contrary to fact, but is expressed through the present subjunctives, perhaps a
case of ungrammatical Latin (cf. G. 8).

quae uero non sunt is a **relative noun clause**, functioning as DO of
apprehendere moliuntur. The subject is still *insipientes* ("fools try to
comprehend/grasp the things that do not truly exist as if they were real").

14 *Qui . . . dulcedinem*: **relative noun clause**, subject of *poterit addiscere*.
Take the first *eorum* with *dulcedinem* and the second *eorum* with *ueritatem*.
sunt is existential: *eorum quae sunt dulcedinem* ("the sweetness of the things
that exist, namely the things that have real existence, that are real").
dulcedinem: DO of *gustaverit* and **antecedent** of *quae sunt*.

16 *quod* + LL **indirect statement** (cf. G. 3.2)

promisissem . . . traderem: negative **contrary to fact condition** with *nisi*. The
condition is mixed: *promisissem* refers to the past while *traderem* refers to the
present.

18 *eo quod*: *eo* is **ablative of cause** ("for this reason"), followed by causal *quod*.
Vir autem dei tristis abscessit: take *tristis* as **subject complement** (i.e.,
predicate adjective) with *abscessit* used as a **linking verb** ("the man of God,
however, went away sad"). When defying the authority of secular rulers,
early Christians were eager to be punished and killed by them, a martyrdom
that would ensure their passage into heaven. The Greek version situates the
Barlaam and Josaphat legend in the great tradition of the early Christian
martyrs, "who resisted sin onto blood" and links them to the monks, the
"martyrs in will," who had struggled in self-discipline and had trodden the
narrow way.[8] Martyrdom in blood was the most coveted type of martyrdom,
while monasticism came second. The sadness of the courtier comes from the
fact that he failed to provoke the king to martyr him. This is a standard motif
in hagiographic narratives: an eager Christian and an official who is reluctant
to mete out capital punishment. Roman officials were often at a loss how to
handle Christians, as Pliny the Younger's famous letter-exchange with the
Emperor Trajan attests.[9]

12 *insipiens, insipientis (adj.)* foolish
despicio, -ere, -spexi, -spectum despise
13 *apprehendo, -ere, -di, -hensum* comprehend, take hold of
molior, -iri, -itus sum try = CL *conor* + **complementary infinitive** (cf. G. 3.3.1)
14 *gusto, -are, -aui, -atum* sip, taste
dulcedo, dinis, f. charm, sweetness

---

8. Woodward and Mattingly (1997) 3.
9. Pliny, *Letters* 10.96–97.

addisco, -ere, -didici learn
ueritas, tatis, f. truth
15 *mysterium, mysterii, n.* mystery
incarnatio, onis, f. incarnation
prosequor, -sequi, -secutus sum tell
16 *concilium, ii, n.* (here) discussion; assembly (CL)
ignis, is, m. fire
carnis, is, f. meat, flesh
17 *ultra (adv.)* further, beyond
perdo, -ere, -didi, -ditum destroy (the adverb *male* adds a colloquial tone)
18 *tristis, -e (adj.)* sad
abscedo, -ere, -cessi, -cessum depart, leave
martyrium, ii, n. martyrdom
perpetior, -peti, -pessus sum endure, suffer

Part 2: The Birth of Prince Josaphat

Josaphat is born and King Avenir consults his astrologers about the future of the child. One astrologer predicts that the newborn will one day become a devout Christian and will renounce his earthly kingdom in favor of a heavenly one. The consultation with astrologers occurs in all versions of the life of the Buddha (cf. Introd. 2.3).

19 Interea, dum rex liberos non haberet, puer ei pulcherrimus nascitur et Iosaphat appellatur. **20** Congregante autem rege infinitam multitudinem ut diis pro ortu pueri immolarent, LV astrologos <u>conuocauit</u>, a quibus quid futurum esset filio suo diligenter <u>quaesiuit</u>. **21** Cunctis autem respondentibus eum magnum in diuitiis et potentia futurum, unus sapientior ex ipsis dixit: **22** "Puer iste qui natus est tibi, o rex, non in tuo erit regno, sed in alio incomparabiliter meliori. **23** Nam illius quam persequeris <u>christianae</u> religionis, ut <u>aestimo</u>, futurus est cultor." **24** Hoc autem non a semet ipso, sed a deo inspirante dixit.

19 *dum+subjunctive*: LL use of *dum* to express cause ("since"). Cf. G. 3.5.2.2.
nascitur . . . appellatur: historical present (A&G 469) which counts as past tense for the rules of **sequence of tenses**.
20 *diis = dis, deis* is dat. pl. of *deus, i,* m.
quid futurum esset: imperfect subjunctive of the First Periphrastic conjugation (A&G 195) in **indirect question** with *quid*. This is how Latin expresses future tense in **indirect questions** where the subjunctive is required ("what would

happen . . ."). Cf. G. 2.4.

21 *futurum*: supply *esse* for the infinitive verb of the **indirect statement** governed by *respondentibus*.

unus sapientior: for *unus* = indefinite article, cf. G. 7.2. *Sapientior* is a **substantive adjective**.

ex ipsis: the meaning is equivalent to **partitive genitive** (cf. G. 5.1).

23 *illius*: read with *religionis*, the **antecedent** of the relative clause *quam persequeris*. *Religionis* is **objective genitive** with *cultor*, **subject complement** (i.e., predicate noun) of implied subject *puer*.

futurus est = *erit* (cf. G. 2.4).

24 *a deo inspirante*: the literal translation of this **ablative of agent** is not very satisfactory because the emphasis falls on the adjectival participle *inspirante*. The loose translation that is more satisfactory would be "from the inspiration of God."

19 *interea (adv.)* in the meantime, meanwhile
liberi, orum, m./f. (pl.) children
pulcher, -a, -um (adj.) beautiful, handsome
nascor, nasci, natus sum be born
20 *congrego, -are, -aui, -atum* gather together
infinitus, -a, -um (adj.) endless, limitless
ortus, us, m. birth, rising
immolo, -are, -aui, -atum sacrifice
astrologus, i, m. astrologer
conuoco, -are, -aui, -atum call together
21 *diuitia, ae, f.* riches, wealth
22 *incomparabiliter (adv.)* incomparably
23 *aestimo = existimo, -are, -aui, -atum* think, consider
cultor, oris, m. worshipper
24 *semet = se* with intensifying suffix *-met*

King Avenir decides to shield his son from witnessing suffering and death. He also mandates that no one should even mention Christ to the prince.

25 Audiens hoc rex et plurimum expauescens in ciuitate seorsum palatium speciosissimum construi fecit et ibi puerum ad habitandum posuit ibique secum iuuenes pulcherrimos collocauit, **26** praecipiens illis ut nec mortem nec senectutem nec infirmitatem uel paupertatem nec aliquid quod possit afferre tristitiam sibi ei nominarent, sed omnia iucunda ei proponerent, quatenus mens eius laetitiis occupata nihil de futuris cogitare posset.
27 Si quem uero ministrantium infirmari contingeret, hunc protinus rex

praecipiebat eici et alium loco eius incolumem subrogari, praecepitque ne sibi de Christo aliquam facerent mentionem.

25 *palatium construi fecit:* LL infinitive for result clause with *fecit* =*iussit* (cf. G. 3.1)
secum: LL use of *se* in lieu of the 3rd person pronoun. CL would have had *cum eō.*
ibi puerum ad habitandum posuit: supply *palatium* with *ad habitandum. Puerum* is the DO of *posuit* ("he placed the boy there to inhabit [it, i.e., the palace]").
26 *quod . . . sibi:* **relative adjectival clause** with *aliquid.* The subjunctive *possit* is used because the relative clause is inside indirect discourse, i.e., **indirect command** (*ut . . . proponerent*).
possit afferre = CL *afferat:* pleonastic use of *possum* + infinitive (cf. G. 2.2.2).
sibi = *ei:* LL use of *sibi*; refers to Prince Josaphat. This is an example of the confusion of reflexive and nonreflexive pronouns in LL (cf. G. 4.1), but in this case, *sibi* is used also in order to avoid the repetition of *ei.*
ei nominarent: correct CL usage (*ei* refers to Prince Josaphat as does *sibi*).
cogitare posset = CL *cogitaret:* subjunctive verb in LL **purpose clause** with *quatenus* (cf. G. 3.5.7) and pleonastic use of *possum* + infinitive (cf. G. 2.2.2).
27 *Si quem* = *si aliquem* (the omission of *ali-* after *num, si, nisi, ne* etc. is a CL feature)
loco eius: "in his place."
praecipiebat . . . praecepit: the change in tense conveys well the fact that the swapping out of servants due to illness was an ongoing procedure, hence the continuous imperfect tense; keeping the mention of Christ from the prince was a single standing order expressed with the perfect tense.
ne sibi = *ei:* refers to Prince Josaphat (cf. G. 4.1).

25 *plurimum (adv.)* much
expauesco, -ere, -paui be terrified, dread
ciuitas, tatis, f. city, town, castle (LL); state, tribe (CL)
seorsum (adv.) separately, apart
palatium, ii, n. palace
speciosus, -a, -um (adj.) beautiful, luxurious
26 *praecipio, -ere, -cepi, -ceptum* order
senectus, tutis, f. old age
infirmitas, tatis, f. illness, weakness
paupertas, tatis, f. poverty
affero, -ferre, -tuli, -latum bring, cause
tristitia, ae, f. sadness, grief

iucundus, -a, -um (adj.) pleasant
nomino, -are, -aui, -atum mention, name
quatenus = CL ut introducing **purpose clause** (cf G. 3.5)
laetitia, ae, f. happiness, joyful occupation
27 *ministro, -are, -aui, -atum* serve
infirmor, -ari, -atus sum be ill
contingit (impers.) it happens
incolumis, -e (adj.) healthy
subrogo, -are, -aui, -atum appoint
protinus (adv.) immediately
eicio, -ere, -ieci, -iectum throw out, eject
mentio, onis, f. mention

Part 3: The Christian Knight and the Word-Mender

*One of the king's knights (*miles*) is a clandestine Christian. The knight offers hospitality to a wounded stranger who turns out to be a word-mender, someone capable of mending relationships when a person says something that he or she later regrets.*

28 Eodem tempore erat cum rege uir quidam christianissimus sed occultus qui inter nobiles regis principes primus erat. **29** Hic dum aliquando cum rege ad uenandum iuisset, hominem quendam pauperem pedem <u>laesum</u> a bestia habentem et in terra iacentem inuenit, a quo rogatur ut se suscipere debeat quia sibi in aliquo forsitan prodesse posset. **30** Cui miles: "Ego quidem te libenter suscipio, sed in quo utilis inueniaris ignoro." **31** Et ille dixit: **32** "Ego homo sum medicus uerborum. **33** Si enim aliquis in uerbis <u>laedatur</u>, congruam scio adhibere medelam". **34** Miles autem quod ille dicebat pro nihilo computauit, propter deum tamen eum suscipiens eius curam egit.

29 *dum . . . iuisset = CL dum* or *cum* + indicative (cf. G. 3.5.2.1).
pedem laesum is DO of the participle *habentem*.
hominem . . . inuenit a quo rogatur ut se suscipere debeat: suscipere debeat = suscipiat. Debeat forms a pleonastic auxiliary verb, common in LL (cf. G. 2.2.3). In translation, *debeat* should be ignored ("he found a man who asked him (the knight) to offer him hospitality"). *Rogatur* is historical present.
30 *in quo utilis inueniaris ignoro:* **indirect question** governed by *ignoro.* Take *utilis* as **subject complement** (i.e., predicate adjective) with subject *tu* and **linking verb** *inueniaris.* In English, the present tense of the subjunctive verb *inueniaris* is awkward and you may want to render it as future ("I do not know

in what you will be found useful").

33 *in uerbis:* LL **ablative of means** expressed through a prepositional phrase (cf. G. 5.1).

scio + infinitive = possum "be able to" (cf. G. 3.3.1).

34 *quod ille dicebat:* **relative noun clause**, DO of *computauit.*

pro nihilo computauit: pro nihilo is the equivalent of the genitive of indefinite value ("calculated to be of no value"). Cf. A&G 417.

curam agere: LL **periphrastic verb** = *curo,* i.e., "take care of someone" (cf. G. 2.2.1).

28 *occultus, -a, -um (adj.)* hidden, in secret
princeps, cipis, m. minister, knight
29 *aliquando (adv.)* at some point in time
uenor, -ari, -atus sum hunt
laedo, -ere, laesi, laesum injure, hurt
suscipio, -ere, -cepi, -ceptum take home, offer hospitality to (+ DO)
forsitan (adv.) perhaps, perchance
prosum, -desse, -fui profit, benefit
30 *libenter (adv.)* with pleasure, gladly
utilis, -e (adj.) useful, helpful
inuenio, -ire, -ueni, -uentum find
ignoro, -are, -aui, -atum not know (CL *nescio*)
32 *medicus, i, m.* doctor, physician
33 *congruus, -a, -um (adj.)* fitting, suitable
medela, ae, f. remedy, cure
34 *computo, -are, -aui, -atum* calculate
curam ago (idiomatic expression) take care of

The knight is the king's favorite. Because of this, the other courtiers are jealous of him. They try to discredit the knight before the king. They go to the king and say: "This knight has not only adopted the Christian faith, but is also trying to gather a crowd and take over your kingdom. If you do not believe us, find out the truth by setting a trap for him. Call him and pretend that you want to leave the kingdom and put on the habit of monks. Tell him that you are regretful of having persecuted them." The king follows the advice and the Christian knight falls into the trap, believing that the king's words are sincere. He responds to the king with tears of joy, praising the king's change of heart.

35 Viri autem quidam inuidi et malitiosi uidentes <u>praedictum</u> principem in tantam gratiam regis esse ipsum apud regem accusauerunt quod non solum ad christianorum fidem declinasset, sed insuper regnum sibi conabatur subripere turbam sollicitans et sibi concilians. **36** "Sed si hoc," inquiunt, "ita esse, o rex, scire desideras, ipsum secreto aduocā et uitam hanc cito finiendam commemorā et idcirco gloriam regni te uelle derelinquere et monachorum habitum assumere asseras quos tamen ignoranter hactenus fueras persecutus et tunc uidebis quid tibi responderit." **37** <u>Quae</u> cum rex omnia ut illi suaserant fecisset, ille doli ignarus perfusus lacrimis propositum regis laudauit et uanitatem mundi rememorans quantocius hoc adimplendum consuluit.

35 *praedictum*: "the aforementioned." This participle is frequently used in LL as the equivalent of the definite article "the" (cf. G. 7.1).
accusauerunt quod: LL **indirect statement** (G. 3.2)
36 *Sed si . . . responderit*: The structure of this long direct speech can be articulated as shown in the Appendix, Example 1. It is a complex periodic sentence with a tricolon of two imperatives (*aduoca, commemora*) and a **jussive subjunctive** (*asseras*) in the apodosis (A&G 512) of the **simple condition**.
finiendam: supply *esse* for the infinitive verb of the **indirect statement** governed by *commemora*. Cf. G. 2.5 for the LL use of the future passive participle instead of the future active participle. Therefore, *finiendam (esse)* here = *finituram esse* ("about to end" rather than "must be ended"). The king is not in a suicidal mood. Instead, he just uses the cliché that says, "life is short, do not waste it on transitory pleasures." By using this well-known topos, he is trying to convince the knight of his change of heart.
ipsum secreto aduoca: *ipsum* refers to the knight.
asseras: the author has switched from the imperatives to **jussive subjunctive**.
fueras persecutus = eras persecutus (cf. G. 2.1).
37 *quae*: **connecting relative**, DO of *fecisset*.
illi: nominative pl, refers to the courtiers who had advised the king to set the trap for the knight.
ille: refers to the knight.
doli: **genitive with the adjective** *ignarus*.
adimplendum: supply *esse* for the **objective infinitive** with *consuluit*.

35 *inuidus, -a, -um (adj.)* jealous, envious
non solum . . . sed not only . . . but also
declino, -are, -aui, -atum favor, be favorably inclined towards
insuper (adv.) additionally, moreover
subripio, -ere, -ripui, -ruptum snatch away, steal
turba, ae, f. crowd
sollicito, -are, -aui, -atum stir up
concilio, -are, -aui, -atum bring over to one's side
36 *inquam* (1st p. sg defective verb; 3rd p. sg *inquit*; 3rd p. pl *inquiunt*) say

secreto (adv.) in secret
finio, -ire, -iui, -itum end, conclude
commemoro, -are, -aui, -atum remember, remind
idcirco (adv.) on that account, therefore
habitus, us, m. attire, clothing
assero, -ere, -serui, -sertum claim, assert
hactenus (adv.) hitherto, up till now
37 *dolus, i, m.* ruse, deceit
lacrima, ae, f. tear
quantocius (LL adv) as quickly as possible, as soon as possible
adimpleo, -ere, -ui, -tum implement
consulo, -ere, -ui, -tum advise + **objective infinitive**

*The king becomes upset with the knight. The knight senses that he had
inadvertently turned the king against himself, but he does not understand
what is wrong. He runs for help to the word-mender to whom he had offered
hospitality in chapter 34.*

38 Quod rex audiens et uerum esse quod illi dixerant credens, furore repletus
est, nihil tamen sibi respondit. **39** Vir autem perpendens quod rex grauiter
uerba sua acceperat, tremens abscessit et medicum se habere uerborum
recolens omnia sibi narrauit.

38 This periodic sentence can be articulated as shown in the Appendix,
Example 2.
nihil tamen sibi respondit: here *sibi = ei* because it refers to the knight and not
to the subject *rex* (cf. G. 4.1).
39 *Vir* is the knight (*miles*) who realizes that he has landed himself in trouble
but cannot understand the king's reaction of anger and therefore goes home
and relates to the *medicus uerborum* what has happened.
perpendens quod: What kind of dependent clause does *quod* introduce?
(cf. G. 3.2).

38 *repleo, -ere, -ui, -etum* fill
39 *perpendeo, -ere, -pendi, -pensum* understand
grauiter (adv.) with irritation
abscedo, -ere, -cedi, -cessum depart
recolo, -ere, -colui, -cultum recall, think over

*The word-mender understands that the king suspects the knight of trying to
usurp his kingdom. Therefore, he devises a plan of action intended to neutralize*

the damage wrought by the scheming courtiers. Just as the jealous courtiers instructed the king in how to set a trap for the clandestine Christian, the word-mender sets up a role-playing act meant to reassure the king that the knight has no intention of usurping his kingdom but is ready to obey him and follow him everywhere, even into the desert.

40 Cui ille: "Notum tibi sit quod rex suspicatur ut propter hoc dixeris quod eius regnum uelis inuadere. **41** Surge igitur et comam tuam tonde et uestimenta abiciens cilicium indue et summo diluculo ad regem ingredere. **42** Cumque rex quid sibi hoc uelit interrogauerit, respondebis: **43** 'Ecce rex, paratus sum sequi te. **44** Nam etsi uia per quam cupis ire difficilis sit, tecum tamen existenti facilis mihi erit. **45** Sicut enim me socium habuisti in prosperis, sic habebis pariter in aduersis. **46** Nunc igitur praesto sum, quid moraris?" **47** Quod cum ille per ordinem fecisset, rex obstupuit et falsarios arguens uirum ampliori honore dotauit.

40 *ille*: refers to the *medicus uerborum* instructing the knight about how to regain the king's trust.
Notum tibi sit quod rex suspicatur ut propter hoc dixeris quod eius regnum uelis inuadere. There are two LL **indirect statements** (G. 3.2) in this sentence alone: *Notum sit quod* ("it should be known that") and *suspicatur ut* ("suspects that"). *quod eius regnum uelis inuadere* is a **causal clause** set up by *propter hoc* ("because of this"). The use of the subjunctive *uelis* is due to the fact that the **causal clause** is inside indirect discourse (A&G 580).
41 *summo diluculo*: "at the crack of dawn."
42 *interrogauerit*: future perfect tense, referring to an action that occurred before the action of the future main verb.
quid sibi hoc uult?: idiomatic expression ("what does this mean?"). The *hoc* in this expression refers to the scene described in the previous sentence, i.e., the knight with shaved head and in rags appearing at the king's door at the crack of dawn.
44 *tecum tamen existenti facilis mihi erit*: the present active participle of *existo* functions as the present active participle of *sum, esse*, which does not have participles (cf. G. 7.3.1). *existenti* is dative sg. with *mihi*; *mihi* is **dative with adjective** *facilis* ("to me while being with you it (the road) will be easy").
45 *socium*: **object complement** with the **factitive verb** *habuisti* ("you had me as companion" or "you considered me a companion").
sic habebis: supply *socium* again.
47 *per ordinem*: "in order," i.e., the knight followed the instructions to the letter.

40 suspicor, -ari, -atus sum mistrust, suspect
41 surgo, -ere, -rexi, -rectum rise
coma, ae, f. hair (of the head)
tondeo, -ere, totondi, tonsum cut, shear
uestimentum, i, n. clothing
cilicium, ii, n. goat's hide vestment
induo, -ere, -dui, dutum put on (when clothing is the DO)
diluculum, i, n. dawn, daybreak
42 quid sibi hoc uult? what does that mean?
45 prosperus, -a, -um (adj.) prosperous (subst. prosperous circumstances)
pariter (adv.) equally
46 praesto (adv.) present
moror, -ari, -atus sum delay, stay
47 obstupesco, -ere, -stupui be astounded
falsarius, ii, m. liar
arguo, -ere, -ui, -utum expose
doto, -are, -aui, -atum endow, gift

Part 4: Prince Josaphat's Chariot Rides

Prince Josaphat wants to see the world and talks to a servant about his desire.
His father Avenir complies and orders the servants to show the prince around,
but he instructs them to shield him from encounters with disease and death. This
episode occurs in all versions of the life of the Buddha as well (cf. Introd. 2.3).

48 Filius igitur eius in palatio educatus ad <u>aetatem</u> adultam peruenit et
in omni sapientia plene edoctus fuit. **49** Admirans igitur cur pater sic
eum reclusisset, unum de conseruis sibi familiariorem secreto de hac re
interrogauit, dicens se in multa <u>maestitia</u> positum pro eo quod sibi foras
egredi non liceret adeo ut nec cibus sibi saperet nec potus. **50** Quod pater
audiens et dolens, equos idoneos parari fecit et choros plaudentes ante eum
mittens, ne quid sibi <u>foedum</u> occurreret diligenter prohibuit.

48 *edoctus fuit* = *edoctus est*: use of *fuit* as an auxiliary verb in the perfect
passive tense is common in CL as well, but is more frequent in LL (cf. G. 2.1).
49 *pro eo*: expresses cause. CL would have used **ablative of cause** *eo* (cf. G. 5.1).
positum (esse) is infinitive in the **indirect statement** governed by *dicens*.
Positus est can be translated as equivalent to *sum, esse* here (cf. G. 7.3.2).
50 *equuos parari fecit*: cf. G. 3.1.
sibi = *ei*: refers to Josaphat (cf. G. 4.1).

48 aetas, tatis, f. age, time of life
plene (adv.) abundantly
edoceo, -ere, -ui educate thoroughly
49 recludo, -ere, -clusi, -clusum shut off
conseruus, i, m. servant
secreto (adv.) secretly
maestitia, ae, f. sadness, sorrow
pro eo = propterea
foras (adv.) outside
cibus, i, m. food, meal
sapio, -ere, -iui have a taste (with "food" as subject)
potus, us, m. drink
50 doleo, -ere, -lui grieve, be sad
chorus, i, m. chorus, troop of dancers
idoneus, -a, -um (adj.) suitable, fitting
plaudo, -ere, plausi, plausum dance, clap
foedus, -a, -um (adj.) bad, nasty
occurro, -currere, -curri, -cursum occur, happen (cf. G. 7.5)

The prince discovers the challenges of human existence, i.e., old age and death. This part of the legend of Barlaam and Josaphat echoes the account of the four sights that Prince Siddhārtha (later the Buddha) saw on his four chariot rides, encountering the various forms of suffering afflicting all humans (birth, aging, sickness, and death).[10] *See also Introd. 2.3.*

51 Praedicto igitur iuuene taliter procedente, quadam uice unus leprosus et unus caecus sibi obuiauerunt. **52** Quos ille uidens et stupens, qui sint et quidnam habeant inquisiuit et ministri dixerunt: **53** "Passiones istae sunt quae hominibus accidunt." **54** Et ille: "Omnibus hominibus haec contingere solent?" **55** Negantibus illis respondit: **56** "Noti sunt igitur qui hoc pati debeant an sic indefinite proueniunt?" **57** Et illi: "Et quis hominum futura scire ualet?" **58** Valde igitur anxius esse coepit pro inconsuetudine rei.
59 Alia autem uice quendam ualde senem rugosam habentem faciem et dorsum incuruatum et cadentibus dentibus balbutiendo loquentem inuenit.
60 Stupefactus discere cupit uisionis miraculum cumque didicisset quod propter annorum multitudinem ad talem statum uenisset, ait: **61** "Et quis est huius finis?" **62** Dicunt ei: "Mors." **63** Et ille: "Estne mors omnium uel aliquorum?" **64** Cumque didicisset omnes mori debere, interrogauit: **65** "In quot annis haec superueniunt?" **66** Et illi: "In octoginta uel centum annis senectus inducitur, deinde mors ipsa subsequitur."

---

10. Lopez and McCracken (2014) 22.

51 *praedictus:* "the aforementioned." This participle is frequently used in LL as the equivalent of the definite article "the" (cf. G. 7.1).

sibi = ei refers to Josaphat (cf. G. 4.1).

52 *qui sint et quidnam habeant:* **indirect questions** with *inquisiuit*.

53 *Passiones istae sunt quae hominibus accidunt:* take *istae* as the subject, referring to the afflictions in the leper and the blind person. The relative clause then modifies the **subject complement** (i.e., predicate noun) *passiones* ("Those are pains that . . .").

56 *noti sunt:* the subject is the **relative noun clause of characteristic** *qui hoc pati debeant* (". . . the people of the sort who would endure this").

pati debeant: LL compound future with *debeo* + infinitive (cf. G. 2.3.1).

proueniunt: the omitted subject is *passiones istae* mentioned in 53. This change of subject is unusual but understandable due to the common meaning of *prouenio* as "happen," a verb that cannot have an animate subject.

58 *pro inconsuetudine rei:* the preposition is causal, "because of the strangeness of the matter" (cf. G. 5.1).

59 *balbutiendo:* **gerund** in the **ablative of means** ("by stammering").

60 *quod:* What kind of dependent clause does *quod* introduce? (cf. G. 3.2).

66 *in octoginta uel centum annis:* **ablative of time** expressed in CL without preposition (cf. G. 5.1).

51 *uice* (abl. sg. of the defective noun *uicis (gen.), uicem (acc.)*) occasion, turn, alternation

leprosus, -a, -um (adj.) one infected with leprosy, leper

caecus, -a, -um (adj.) blind

obuio, -are, -aui, -atum come towards (+ dat)

52 *stupeo, -ere, stupui* be astounded

quisnam, quidnam = quis, quid

inquiro, -ere, -quisiui, -quisitum ask

53 *passio, onis, f.* pain, suffering

54 *contingit (impers.)* happens

55 *nosco, -ere, noui, notum* know

56 *indefinite (adv.)* randomly

prouenio, -ire, -ueni, -uentum come to pass, happen

57 *ualeo, -ere, ualui = possum, posse, potui* (cf. G. 3.3.1)

58 *anxius, -a, -um (adj.)* anxious, uneasy

inconsuetudo, tudinis, f. unusualness, strangeness

59 *rugosus, -a, -um (adj.)* full of wrinkles

dorsum, i, n. back

incuruo, -are, -aui, -atum bend

balbutio, -ire stammer, babble

60 stupefacio, -ere, -feci, -factum stupefy
disco, -ere, didici learn
uisio, onis, f. sight, seen object
status, us, m. condition
65 superuenio, -ire, -ueni, -uentum come about, happen
66 senectus, tutis, f. old age
induco, -ere, -duxi, -ductum bring on

Part 5: Barlaam Arrives and Starts to Instruct Prince Josaphat

The prince, puzzled by his new discoveries, is shocked and saddened but feigns happiness before his father. The Christian hermit Barlaam, sensing that the prince is in a receptive state of mind, arrives at his private palace disguised as a merchant.

67 Haec igitur iuuenis frequenter in corde suo recogitans in multa desolatione erat, sed coram patre laetitiam praetendebat, plurimum desiderans in huiusmodi dirigi et doceri. **68** Igitur quidam monachus uitā et opinione perfectus habitans in deserto terrae Sennaar, nomine Barlaam, haec quae circa filium regis agebantur per spiritum cognouit et mercatoris habitum sumens ad ciuitatem illam deuenit.

68 *Senaar*: indeclinable noun and place name for the land between the Tigris and Euphrates, known at the time as Chaldea or Babylonia.[11] We know that its case is genitive singular because it is in apposition to the genitive noun *terrae*. *nomine Barlaam*: Barlaam is a nominative noun in apposition (A&G 282) to *monachus*; *nomine* is **ablative of specification (respect)**, i.e., "Barlaam by name."

67 desolatio, onis, f. despair
coram (prep + abl) in front of
praetendo, -ere, -tendi, -tentum present, feign
huiusmodi (indecl. pronoun) such things, this (cf. G. 4.4)
dirigo, -ere, -rexi, -rectus guide
68 monachus, i, m. monk
opinio, onis, f. reputation
perficio, -ere, -feci, -fectus accomplish, complete
desertum, i n. desert (LL)

---

11. Woodward and Mattingly (1997) 624 (index).

circa = circum (prep +acc)
mercator, oris, m. trader, merchant
habitus, us, m. attire, clothing
ciuitas, tatis, f. city, town, castle (LL); state, tribe (CL)
deuenio, -ire, -ueni, -uentum arrive

*Barlaam asks the tutor of the prince for access to the young man. To trick
the tutor, Barlaam claims that he has a magic stone that does miracles for
individuals with pure character and pure eyes. However, the stone blinds anyone
with impure eyes. He says that he wants to show the stone to Josaphat. The tutor
decides not to take the risk of looking at the stone himself and lets Barlaam into
the presence of the prince.*

69 Accedensque <u>paedagogo</u> filii regis locutus est dicens: **70** "Ego, cum
negotiator sim, lapidem pretiosum uenalem habeo, qui <u>caecis</u> lumen tribuit,
surdis aures aperit, mutos loqui facit, insipientibus sapientiam infundit.
71 Nunc igitur duc me ad filium regis ut hunc sibi tradam." **72** Cui ille:
"Videris homo <u>maturae prudentiae</u>, sed uerba tua <u>prudentiae</u> non concordant.
73 Verumtamen cum lapidum notitiam habeam, ipsum lapidem mihi
ostende et, si talis ut asseris fuerit comprobatus, a filio regis honores maximos
consequeris." **74** Ad quem ille: "Lapis meus hanc insuper habet uirtutem, quia
qui non habet sanam oculorum aciem et qui non seruat integram castitatem,
si forte illum aspexerit, ipsam uirtutem quam habet uisibilem perdit. **75** Ego
autem medicinalis artis non expers uideo te sanos oculos non habere, filium
autem regis audiui pudicum esse et oculos pulcherrimos et sanos habere."
76 Cui ille: "Si sic est, noli mihi ostendere, quia et oculos sanos non habeo et
in peccatis sordesco."

71 *sibi = ei:* refers to the prince (cf. G. 4.1). The speaker is Barlaam disguised
as merchant.
73 *notitiam habeam:* for the periphrastic use of *habeo,* cf. G. 2.2.1.
fuerit comprobatus = erit comprobatus: the use of *fuerit* as the auxiliary verb of
the future perfect tense is common in CL as well, but is more frequent in LL
(cf. G. 2.1).
74 *quia:* the Latin translation follows the Greek closely, producing an instance
of nongrammatical Latin (cf. G. 8). This *quia* = CL **result clause** with ut +
subjunctive ("my stone in addition has this property, namely that . . ." Neither
CL nor LL has result clauses with *quia.* LL has result clauses with *quod* (cf. G.
3.5.4).
qui non habet sanam oculorum aciem et qui non seruat integram castitatem:
these two **relative noun clauses** function as subjects of *aspexerit* and *perdit.*

The person who does not have healthy (spiritual) vision (*sanam oculorum aciem*) and does not keep his chastity intact loses his or her seeing capacity (*uirtutem uisibilem*) upon glancing at the stone. This interpretation is most in keeping with the periodic nested clauses in this complex sentence. I disagree with Ryan's translation that makes the stone lose its magical properties when a person with bad vision and lacking chastity beholds it.[12] Since the Latin translations come from a Greek original, it is the Greek version that can clarify the occasional awkwardly phrased passages as this one. The Greek version here says: "This exceedingly precious gem, amongst these powers and virtues, possesses this property besides. It cannot be seen out of hand, save by one whose eyesight is strong and sound and his body pure and thoroughly undefiled. If any man, lacking in these two good qualities, do rashly gaze upon this precious stone, he shall, I suppose lose even the eyesight he has, and his wits as well."[13]

si forte illum aspexerit: illum refers to the stone. The stone would blind a person lacking spiritual vision and chaste character.

ipsam uirtutem: the pronoun *ipsam* = the definite article, i.e., "the capacity" (cf. G. 4.3).

ipsam uirtutem quam habet uisibilem: "the seeing capacity, which he (the person beholding the stone) has." This is a clumsy Latin translation of the Greek *optikē dynamis* ("seeing capacity").[14]

76 *noli ostendere*: **negative command**, formed with *noli* + inf. (CL) "do not show."

69 *paedagogus, i, m.* teacher (LL from Greek *paedagogos*)
70 *negotiator, oris, m.* dealer, trader
lapis, idis, m. stone, rock
uenalis, -e (adj.) for hire, open to sale
caecus, -a, -um (adj.) blind
surdus, -a, -um (adj.) deaf
aperio, -ire, aperui, apertum open
mutus, -a, -um (adj.) dumb, lacking speech
73 *notitia, ae, f.* knowledge
assero, -ere, -serui, -sertum say, assert
comprobo, -are, -aui, -atum prove
consequor, -sequi, -secutus sum receive

---

12. Ryan (1993) 358 translates: "The stone has still another power, namely, that if someone who does not enjoy good eyesight and does not live a chaste life inspects the stone, the stone loses all its powers."
13. Slightly modified translation of Woodward and Mattingly (1997) 65–67.
14. Woodward and Mattingly (1997) 64.

74 insuper (adv.) in addition, moreover
uirtus, tutis, f. (here) property, capacity (translation of Greek *dynamis*)
sanus, -a, -um (adj.) sound, healthy
acies, ei, f. sight
castitas, tatis, f. purity, chastity
aspicio, -ere, -spexi, -spectum look at
uisibilis, -e (adj.) visible
perdo, -ere, -didi, -ditum lose irrecoverably
75 expers, expertis (adj.) lacking, inexperienced in (+ gen)
pudicus, -a, -um (adj.) chaste, modest
76 sordesco, -ere, -dui, -ditum be soiled

5.1 BARLAAM'S FIRST PARABLE: THE HERALD OF DEATH AND THE FOUR CHESTS

Barlaam meets the prince and starts instructing him. He tells him a series of parables. His first parable is designed to praise the prince for receiving a humble person like Barlaam with hospitality. The parable tells the story of another king who respectfully bowed before some poor persons dressed in rags.

77 Nuntians igitur hoc filio regis ipsum ad eum quantocius introduxit. **78** Cum ergo introductus fuisset et rex eum reuerenter suscepisset, ait Barlaam: **79** "Hoc, rex, bene fecisti, quia de foris paruitati apparenti non attendisti: **80** nam rex quidam magnus in curru deaurato procedens, cum quibusdam attritas uestes indutis et macie attenuatis obuiasset, continuo de curru exiliens ad eius[15] pedes procidens ipsos adorauit et surgens in oscula eius ruit.

77 *ipsum*: refers to Barlaam disguised as merchant.
ad eum: refers to Prince Josaphat.
78 *introductus fuisset* = *introductus esset*: CL also uses *fuissem* instead of *essem* as the auxiliary verb to form the pluperfect passive subjunctive, but this is more common in LL (cf. G. 2.1).
rex eum: Prince Josaphat was called *filius regis* in 77 and is called *rex* here (an inconsistency); *eum* refers to Barlaam disguised as merchant.
79 *de foris*: LL preposition + adverb (cf. G. 5.2). It modifies the dative sg. present active participle *apparenti. LL apparet = CL uidetur* (cf. G. 7.7) "because you did not pay attention to my status, appearing (seeming) low on the outside."

---

15. The manuscript here reads "eius," but the passage is corrupt. The same is true about the next "eius." Both should read "eorum."

80 *cum quibusdam:* introducing a *cum*-clause, even though *cum* is immediately followed by the ablative *quibusdam.*

quibusdam: **dative with compound verb** *obuiasset.*

attritas uestes indutis: uestes is Greek accusative (A&G 397b) with *indutis* in the middle voice. The participle has a reflexive sense ("covered with ragged clothes," i.e., "having covered themselves in ragged clothes"). The Greek accusative in CL occurs only in poetry.

eius = eorum: refers to the people dressed in ragged clothes.

77 *quantocius (adv.)* as quickly as possible
introduco, -ere, -duxi, -ductus lead in, bring in
78 *reuerenter (adv.)* respectfully
suscipio, -ere, -cepi, -ceptum receive, offer hospitality to (+ DO)
79 *de foris (adv., often spelled as one word, deforis)* externally, on the outside (cf. G. 5.2)
paruitas, tatis, f. insignificance, low status
attendo, -ere, -di, -tentum pay attention to, look to (+ dat)
80 *currus, us, m.* chariot
deauro, -are, -aui, -atum gild
attritus, -a, -um (adj.) ragged
uestis, is, f. clothing, garment
induo, -ere, -dui, -dutum dress, clothe
macies, iei, f. leaness, poverty
attenuo, -are, -aui, -atum make thin, weaken
obuio, -are, -aui, -atum meet
continuo (adv.) immediately
exilio, -ire, -lui leap forth
procido, -ere, -cidi fall prostrate
adoro, -are, -aui, -atum worship, adore
surgo, -ere, -rexi, -rectum rise
osculum i, n. kiss, mouth
ruo, -ere, rui hurry, rush

In Barlaam's parable, the courtiers complain about the king's behavior to his brother who chastises the king for his unconventional behavior.

81 Proceres autem eius indigne hoc ferentes, sed regem super hoc arguere formidantes, fratri retulerunt quomodo rex magnificentiae regali indigna fecisset, frater autem regem super hoc redarguit.

81 *arguere formidantes:* LL infinitive of the goal (cf. G. 3.3.2) "afraid to reproach him."
indigna: neuter plural **substantive adjective** ("things unworthy of . . .").
magnificentiae regali: **dative with adjective** *indigna.*

81 *procer, eris, m.* nobleman
indigne (adv.) indignantly *(indigne ferre* "be upset about the DO")
arguo, -ere, -gui, -gutum reproach, blame
formido, -are, -aui, -atum fear
refero, -ferre, rettuli, relatum report
quomodo (question word) how + **indirect question**
indignus, -a, -um (adj.) unworthy of, unbecoming to + dat (CL + abl)
redarguo, -ere, -gui blame, reproach

The king in Barlaam's parable gives his brother a practical lesson. He shows to his brother that his reverence for the poor persons was dictated by fear of God because to him, the poor persons were like messengers of God to be feared in the same way as his brother feared the herald of death.

82 Erat autem regi consuetudo quod, quando aliquis morti tradendus erat, rex ante eius ianuam praeconem cum tuba ad hoc deputata mittebat. **83** Vespere igitur ueniente ante fratris ianuam tubam sonari fecit. **84** Quod ille audiens et de sua salute desperans totam noctem insomnem duxit et testamentum fecit, mane autem facto indutus nigris uestibus cum uxore et filiis ad fores palatii lugens accessit. **85** Quem rex ad se ingredi faciens dixit: **86** "O stulte, si praeconem fratris tui, cui nihil te deliquisse cognoscis, adeo timuisti, quomodo praecones domini mei, in quem adeo peccaui, timere non debeam, qui sonabilius mihi tubā mortem significant et terribilem iudicis aduentum denuntiant?"

82 *consuetudo quod:* LL **noun result clause** with *quod* + indicative = CL *ut* + subjunctive (cf. G. 3.5.5).
quando = CL ***cum* temporal** (cf. G. 3.5.6).
83 *fecit* and **85** *faciens:* cf. G. 3.1.
84 *ille:* refers to the king's brother who thinks that he is condemned to death for criticizing the king.
noctem . . . duxit: "spent the night."
86 This sentence has a periodic structure that can be articulated for easier translation as shown in the Appendix, Example 3.
timere non debeam: LL compound future with *debeo* + infinitive (cf. G. 2.3.1), i.e., "shall/should I not fear."

tubā: **ablative of comparison** with the comparative adverb *sonabilius* ("he heralds of the Lord signal death and the horrifying approach of the judge more loudly *than* a trumpet can"). The heralds of the Lord are compared to the trumpet (*tuba*) mentioned above in chapter 82.

82 *consuetudo, inis, f.* custom
praeco, onis, m. herald
tuba, ae, f. trumpet
ad hoc for this (purpose)
deputo, -are, -aui, -atum dispatch, designate
83 *uesper, eris, m.* evening
sono, -are, -aui, -atum make a sound
84 *salus, salutis, f.* health, safety
despero, -are, -aui, -atum be in despair, give up hope
testamentum, i, n. death will
mane (indecl.) morning
lugeo, -ere, luxi, luctum mourn
85 *ingredior, -gredi, -gressus* sum walk, advance
86 *delinquo, -ere, -liqui, -lictum* commit crime against someone (+ dat)
quomodo (question word) how? why?
pecco, -are, -aui, -atum sin
sonabilius (comparative adv. of sonabilis, -e) more loudly
significo, -are, -aui, -atum announce, signal

The king in Barlaam's parable gives the members of his court a practical lesson too. He brings in four chests with deceptive exteriors to teach his noblemen to look beyond first appearances. Barlaam uses this story to compliment the prince for acting like the king of the parable who honored the homely poor persons in ragged clothes.

Shakespeare adapted this popular story in his play "The Merchant of Venice," where he made the four chests into three caskets (gold, silver, lead), but the message is the same: of the three suitors that come for the hand of lady Portia, the one who chose the lead casket received her in marriage. The ones who chose the golden and the silver caskets respectively were rejected. The love of her heart Bassanio chose the lead casket, and when he opened it he read the following message inscribed on a scroll:

You that choose not by the view,
Chance as fair and choose as true!
Since this fortune falls to you,
Be content and seek no new,

If you be well pleased with this
And hold your fortune for your bliss,
Turn you where your lady is
And claim her with a loving kiss.[16]

87 Deinde quattuor capsas fieri iussit et duas earum extrinsecus auro undique operiri et ossibus mortuorum putridis impleri, duas uero pice liniri et gemmis et margaritis pretiosis impleri fecit. **88** Vocansque illos magnates quos sciebat querimoniam apud fratrem deposuisse, quatuor illas capsas ante eos posuit et <u>quae</u> pretiosiores essent inquisiuit. **89** Illi uero duas deauratas magni esse pretii, reliquas uero uilis pretii esse indicauerunt. **90** <u>Praecepit</u> igitur rex deauratas aperiri et continuo inde <u>foetor</u> intolerabilis exhalauit. **91** Quibus rex: "<u>Haec</u> illis similes sunt, qui gloriosis uestibus sunt amicti, intus uero immunditia uitiorum pleni." **92** Deinde alias aperiri fecit et ecce odor inde mirabilis exhalauit. **93** Quibus rex: "<u>Istae</u> illis pauperrimis quos honoraui similes sunt qui, etsi uilibus uestimentis operiantur, intus tamen omni uirtutum odore resplendent; **94** uos autem solum <u>quae</u> de foris sunt attenditis et <u>quae</u> deintus sunt non consideratis." **95** Secundum igitur illum regem tu quoque fecisti bene suscipiens me."

87 *fecit*: cf. G. 3.1. See another example in 92.
88 *quae* introduces **indirect question** with *inquisivit*.
89 *magni pretii* and *uilis pretii*: genitives of indefinite value (A&G 417) translated as "of great value," "of little value."
94 *quae de foris sunt*: **relative noun clause**, DO of *attenditis* ("you pay attention to the things which are outside"). *De foris* and *deintus* are LL compound adverbs (cf. G. 5.2).

87 *capsa, ae, f.* chest, casket
extrinsecus (adv.) on the outside, externally
operio, -ire, operui, opertum cover, hide
putridus, -a, -um (adj.) decayed, rotten
pix, picis, f. pitch, tar
linio, -ire, -iui, -itum smear, seal
gemma, ae, f. jewel
margarita, ae, f. pearl
pretiosus, -a, -um (adj.) valuable, expensive
88 *magnas, atis, m.* nobleman, baron
querimonia, ae, f. complaint

---

16. Bassanio in Act III, Scene 2 of the *Merchant of Venice* (open source Shakespeare on the Web).

89 pretium, ii, n. value, worth
90 praecipio, -ere, -cepi, -ceptum instruct, order
aperio, -ire, aperui, apertum uncover, open
continuo (adv.) immediately, at once
foetor, oris, m. stench, bad smell
exhalo, -are, -aui, -atum breathe out, pour out
91 amicio, -ire, -mixi, -mictum clothe, dress
intus (adv.) within, on the inside
immunditia, ae, f. dirtiness, foulness
uitium, ii, n. vice, sin
93 etsi (conj.) although
resplendeo, -ere, -dui shine
94 deintus (adv.) within (similar to *deforis/de foris*, cf. G. 5.2)
considero, -are, -aui, -atum examine
95 secundum (prep. + acc) in accordance with, following after
suscipio, -ere, -cepi, -ceptum receive, offer hospitality to (+ DO)

5.2. BARLAAM'S SECOND PARABLE: THE ARCHER AND THE NIGHTINGALE

The story of the archer and the nightingale is supposed to illustrate the foolishness of idol-worship. However, it is a universal story that could lend itself to a number of interpretations about the gullability of humans whose greed makes them easy prey to deception and false promises.

96 Incipiens igitur Barlaam <u>coepit</u> ei de mundi creatione et hominis <u>praeuaricatione</u> ac filii dei incarnatione, passione et resurrectione longum sermonem retexere necnon et de die iudicii et retributione bonorum et malorum multa ponere et seruientes <u>idolis</u> plurimum exprobrare ac de eorum fatuitate tale exemplum proferre dicens: **97** "Sagittarius quidam auiculam paruam nomine philomenam capiens, cum uellet eam occidere, uox data est <u>philomenae</u> et ait: **98** "Quid tibi proderit, o homo, si me occideris? **99** Neque enim uentrem tuum de me implere ualebis, sed, si me dimittere uelles, tria tibi mandata darem; <u>quae</u> si diligentius conseruares, magnam inde utilitatem consequi posses." **100** Ille uero ad eius loquelam stupefactus promisit quod eam dimitteret si <u>haec</u> sibi mandata proferret.

96 *coepit . . . retexere:* Barlaam's sermon or discourse about the creation of the world, etc., has been told many times, hence the choice of the verb *retexo* here. *seruientes:* substantive use of the participle with **dative object** *idolis* ("people worshipping idols"). Cf. G. 3.6.

multa ponere: take *pono* to mean "present, posit" ("began . . . to present many things").

99 *dimittere uelles:* LL compound future with *uolo* + infinitive (cf. G. 2.3.2).

quae: **connecting relative**, DO of *conseruares.* Maggioni (2007) prints a comma before *quae,* which results in ungrammatical Latin (cf. G. 8).

inde = ex eis, i.e., from the mandates (cf. G. 7.10).

consequi posses = CL *consequereris:* LL pleonastic use of *possum* + infinitive (cf. G. 2.2.2).

100 *quod* + LL **indirect statement** after *promisit* (cf. G. 3.2).

haec: agrees with *mandata* ("these mandates")

sibi = ei: refers to the archer (cf. G. 4.1). The subject of *proferret* is the nightingale.

96 *mundus, i, m.* world
praeuaricatio, onis, f. transgression
sermo, onis, f. sermon (LL); discourse, conversation (CL)
retexo, -ere, -texui, -textum retell
necnon (adv.) and also
iudicium, i, n. judgment
retributio, onis, f. reward
seruio, -ire, -iui, -itum worship (LL); serve, be slave to (+ dat) (CL)
idolum, i, n. idol, image of pagan deity (LL from Greek *eidolon*)
plurimum (adv.) most of all
exprobro, -are, -aui, -atum reproach
fatuitas, tatis, f. foolishness
profero, -ferre, -tuli, -latum bring forward, offer
97 *sagittarius, ii, m.* archer
auicula, ae, f. small bird
philomena, ae, f. nightingale
98 *prosum, -desse, -fui* benefit (+ dat)
occido, -ere, -cidi, -cisum kill
99 *impleo, -ere, -eui, -etum* fill in, complete
ualeo, ualere, ualui = possum, posse, potui (cf. G. 3.3.1)
mandatum, i, n. mandate, commandment
diligentius = diligenter (adv.) carefully
conseruo, -are, -aui, -atum preserve, maintain
utilitas, tatis, f. profit, advantage
consequor, -sequi, -secutus sum receive
100 *loquela, ae, f.* speech, utterance
stupefacio, -ere, -feci, -factum strike dumb, stun
profero, -ferre, -tuli, -latum reveal

The nightingale gives three mandates to the archer who fails to follow them. His gullibility and foolishness are revealed.

101 Et illa: "Numquam rem <u>quae</u> apprehendi non potest apprehendere studeas; **102** de re perdita et irrecuperabili nunquam doleas; **103** uerbum incredibile nunquam credas. **104** <u>Haec</u> tria custodi et bene tibi erit." **105** Ille autem, ut promiserat, eam dimisit, philomena igitur per aera uolitans dixit ei: **106** "<u>Vae</u> tibi, homo, quam malum consilium habuisti et quam magnum thesaurum hodie perdidisti! **107** Est enim in meis uisceribus margarita <u>quae</u> struthionis ouum sua uincit magnitudine." **108** Quod ille audiens ualde contristatus est quod eam dimiserit et eam apprehendere conabatur dicens: **109** "Veni in domum meam et omnem tibi humanitatem exhibebo et honorifice te dimittam." **110** Cui philomena: "Nunc pro certo cognoui te fatuum esse. **111** Nam ex <u>his quae</u> tibi dixi nullum profectum habuisti, quia et de me perdita et irrecuperabili doles et me temptasti capere, cum nequeas meo itinere pergere, et insuper margaritam tam grandem in meis uisceribus esse credidisti, cum ego tota ad magnitudinem oui struthionis non ualeam pertingere." **112** Sic ergo stulti sunt illi qui confidunt in <u>idolis</u> quia plasmatos a se adorant et custoditos a se custodes suos appellant."

106 *quam malum consilium:* here *quam* is an adverb "how" ("how bad of a plan"), Cf. A&G 217c.
108 *quod eam dimiserit:* LL **indirect statement** (cf. G. 3.2).
111 *his* (abl. pl.) appears as *hiis* in the original. The form arises from confusion with *iis/eis* (see G. 1.2).
111 *temptasti:* syncopated form of *temptauisti.*
ualeam + **complementary infinitive** (cf. G. 3.3.1).
112 *confidunt in idolis: confido* takes **dative object** in CL. The use of the prepositional phrase with this verb is a LL feature. There is also a grammatical inconsistency regarding gender because *idolum* is neuter sg. while the participles *plasmatos* and *custoditos* that modify implied *idola* are masculine pl. *plasmatos* and *custoditos:* substantive participles. The substantives function as DOs of *adorant* and *appellant* respectively. Both are modified by their own **ablative of agent** (*a se*). Cf. G. 3.6.
112. The conclusion with the condemnation of idol-worship does not sit well with the rest of the parable. This shows that the attack on idol-worshippers was a later add-on to an older story. For the not always seemless Christianization of the legend, see Introd. 2.3.

101 studeo, -ere, -ui strive after, be eager to
102 perdo, -ere, -didi, -ditum lose, destroy

irrecuperabilis, -e (adj.) unrecoverable
104 *custodio, -ire, -iui, -itum* take heed, guard
105 *aer, aeris, n.* air
uolito, -are, -aui, -atum fly
106 *uae! (interj.)* woe!
quam (adv.) how
thesaurus, i, m. treasure
107 *uiscus, eris, n.* (usually pl.) entrails
margarita, ae, f. pearl
struthio, onis, m. ostrich
ouum, i, n. egg
108 *ualde (adv.) very*, intensely
contristo, -are, -aui, -atum sadden
109 *exhibeo, -ere, -bui, -bitum* present, produce
honorifice (adv.) honorably
110 *certus, a, um* certain (*pro certo* for certain, for sure)
cognosco, -ere, -noui, -nitum learn
fatuus, -a, -um (adj.) foolish
111 *profectus, us, m.* profit, benefit
tempto, -are, -aui, -atum try
nequeo, -ire, -iui, -itum not be able
pergo, -ere, -rexi, -rectum go, follow
pertingo, -ere reach, extend
112 *stultus, -a, -um (adj.)* foolish
idolum, i, n. idol, image of pagain deity (LL from Greek *eidolon*)
plasmo, -are, -aui, -atum form, make
adoro, -are, -aui, -atum worship, adore
custos, odis, m. guardian

5.3. BARLAAM'S THIRD PARABLE: THE MAN IN THE WELL

Barlaam's third parable illustrates the condition of those who are absorbed in the temporary pleasures of this world. The parable compares them to a man who fell into a deep well. Surrounded by danger on all sides, he noticed a drip of honey trickling down from a branch above and that sweetness made him forget his predicament. The allegory predates Buddhism. It is included in the Mahābhārata[17] and Pantschatantra[18] and is also found in Jain writings.[19] It was one of the most influential parables in the legend (cf. figs. 1 and 2 and Introd. 1.1 and 3.3).

17. Lopez and McCracken (2014) 100.
18. Almond (1987) 395.
19. Almond (1987) 398.

113 Coepitque contra fallacem mundi delectationem et uanitatem multa
disputare et plura ad hoc exempla adducere dicens: **114** "Qui delectationes
corporales desiderant et animas suas fame mori permittunt, similes sunt
cuidam homini qui, dum a facie unicornis ne ab eo deuoraretur uelocius
fugeret, in quoddam barathrum magnum cecidit. **115** Dum autem caderet,
manibus arbustulam quandam apprehendit et in base quadam lubrica et
instabili pedes fixit. **116** Respiciens uero uidit duos mures, unum album
et alium nigrum, incessanter radicem arbustulae quam apprehenderat
corrodentes et iam prope erat ut ipsam absciderent. **117** In fundo autem
baratri uidit draconem terribilem spirantem ignem et aperto ore ipsum
deuorare cupientem, super basem uero, ubi pedes tenebat, uidit quatuor
aspidum capita inde prodeuntia. **118** Eleuans autem oculos uidit exiguum
mellis de ramis illius arbustulae oblitusque periculi in quo undique positus
erat, se ipsum dulcedini illius modici mellis totum dedit.

113 *plura ad hoc exempla:* one of many discontinuous noun-phrases in this
text (cf. G. 6.3). Translate as "many examples to this (effect)."
114 *Qui . . . permittunt:* **relative noun clause**, subject of the main verb *sunt*
("those who; whoever . . ."). This sentence contains nested clauses that can be
articulated for easier translation as shown in Appendix, Example 4.
dum + subjunctive *fugeret* = CL *cum/dum* + indicative "when/while" (cf. G.
3.5.2).
unicornis: cf. fig. 2 for a drawing of the unicorn in a manuscript from the early
1300s. A unicorn-like animal with one horn can be found on seals from the
Indus Valley civilization as early as 2500 BCE.[20] This legendary animal became
symbol of the incarnation of Christ in the Middle Ages. The figure was also
used in heraldry to signify independence since the animal was believed to be
very difficult to capture. According to popular lore, it would only surrender to
a virgin. In our legend, the unicorn symbolizes death.
quodam = *quoddam* (accusative singular neuter).
116 *iam prope erat ut . . . :* the **noun result clause** that begins with *ut* is the
subject of the impersonal expression *prope erat* ("it was already almost the
case that . . .").
118 *exiguum mellis:* substantive use of the adjective *exiguum* ("a little bit")
with **partitive genitive** *mellis.*

113 *fallax, fallacis (adj.)* false, deceitful
delectatio, onis, f. pleasure, delight
disputo, -are, -aui, -atum discuss, argue

---

20. Kenoyer (1998) 87.

114 *corporalis, -e (adj.)* bodily
desidero, -are, -aui, -atum wish for
anima, ae, f. soul
fames, is, f. hunger
morior, mori, mortuus sum die
unicornis, is, m. unicorn
deuoro, -are, -aui, -atum devour, eat up
uelox, uelocis (adj.) quick
barathrum, i, n. abyss, well (LL from Greek *barathron*)
cado, -ere, cecidi, casum fall
115 *arbustula, ae, f.* shrub, small tree
basis, is, f. platform, foothold (from Greek *basis*)
lubricus, -a, -um (adj.) slippery
instabilis, -e (adj.) unstable
pes, pedis, m. foot
figo, -ere, fixi, fixus fix, set
116 *respicio, -ere, -spexi, -spectum* look back
mus, muris, m. mouse
incessanter (adv.) ceaselessly
radix, icis, f. root
corrodo, -ere, -rosi, -rosum gnaw away
prope (adv.) nearly
abscido, -ere, -scidi, -scisum hew away, cut away
117 *fundus, i, m.* ground
draco, onis, m. dragon
spiro, -are, -aui, -atum breathe
aperio, -ire, aperui, apertum open
aspis, idis, f. asp
prodeo, -dire, -di(u)i, -ditum come out, spring up
118 *eleuo, -are, -aui, -atum* lift up, raise
exiguus, -a, -um (adj.) small, little
mel, mellis, n. honey
ramus, i, m. branch
obliuiscor, -uisci, oblitus sum forget (+ gen.)
periculum, i, n. trial, test
undique (adv.) everywhere, completely
dulcedo, inis, f. sweetness
modicum, i, n. small amount

Interpretation of the parable about the man in the well. Consult figure 2 for the most detailed illustration of the parable, included in a Latin manuscript from the early 1300s, originating a few decades after Jacobus de Voragine's death.

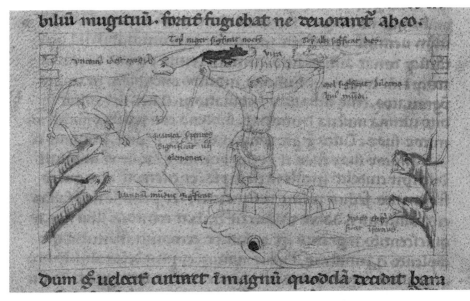

Fig. 2. Detailed illustration of the man in the well parable in "a Latin version of *Liber Barlaam et Josaphat servorum Dei* dating from the early 1300s" (Aavitsland 2012: 112). BAV, ms. Ottob. lat. 269. fol. 35v.

© 2017 Biblioteca Apostolica Vaticana, by permission of Biblioteca Apostolica Vaticana, with all rights reserved.

119 Unicornis autem mortis tenet figuram <u>quae</u> hominem semper persequitur et apprehendere cupit, baratrum uero mundus est omnibus malis plenus. **120** Arbustula uniuscuiusque uita est <u>quae</u> per horas diei et noctis quasi per murem album et nigrum incessanter consumitur et incisioni appropinquat. **121** Basis quatuor aspidum corpus ex quatuor elementis compositum, quibus inordinatis corporis compago dissoluitur. **122** Draco terribilis os inferni cunctos deuorare cupiens, dulcedo ramusculi delectatio fallax mundi, per quam homo seducitur ut periculum suum minime intueatur."

119 *tenet figuram*: "has the allegorical meaning."
121–122 Supply *est* as the verb in each main clause (as expressed in 120). The meaning of each element mentioned in the parable (*arbustula, draco, basis, dulcedo*) is explained next.
121 *basis quattuor aspidum*: the platform where the man landed is guarded by the four asps, so *aspidum* is **genitive of possession**, indicating that the platform belongs to the snakes. The genitives, however, can also be interpreted as the genitive of material (A&G 344), thus making the man's situation even

more precarious. The only stable footing that he has under his feet consists of four vipers (asps).

corpus ex quatuor elementis compositum: supply *est*; *corpus* refers to the human body. The concept of the four elements (water, fire, air, and earth) that make up the physical body is found not only in Indian scriptures[21] but also in the writings of the 5th-century BCE Greek philosopher Empedocles.[22] This compressed sentence implies that while the body is alive, the four elements are in good order, i.e., they are in harmony with each other, but when this order ceases to exist (*quibus inordinatis*), the body decomposes.

quibus inordinatis . . . dissoluitur: **abl of cause** ("because of the lack of order in them . . . the compound of the body is dissolved").

119 *teneo, -ere, tenui, tentum* hold, have
figura, ae f. symbol, allegory, allegorical meaning
120 *unusquisque (pron.)* each and everyone/everything
incisio, onis, f. incision, cutting
appropinquo, -are, -aui, -atum approach, come near to (+ dat)
121 *basis, is, f.* platform, foothold (from Greek *basis*)
compono, -ere, -posui, -positum compose, make up
inordinatus, -a, -um (adj.) disordered
compago, inis, f. order, structure
dissoluo, -ere, -lui, -lutum dissolve, destroy
122 *infernus, i, m.* hell
ramusculus, i, m. little twig
seduco, -ere, -duxi, -ductum lead astray
minime (adv.) not at all
intueor, -tueri, -tuitus sum see, have insight into

5.4 BARLAAM'S FOURTH PARABLE: THE MAN AND HIS THREE FRIENDS

A man had three friends. Two of them whom he favored most abandoned him in his time of need.

123 Addidit quoque dicens: **124** "Similes sunt iterum mundi amatores homini qui tres amicos habuit. **125** Quorum unum plus quam se, secundum tantum quantum se, tertium minus quam se et quasi nihil dilexit. **126** In magno itaque periculo positus et a rege citatus cucurrit ad primum amicum eius auxilium <u>quaerens</u> et qualiter eum semper dilexerit commemorans. **127** Cui ille: "Nescio quis sis, o homo, habeo alios amicos cum quibus me hodie

---

21. Gupta (2012) 64.
22. Diels-Kranz (1966) fr. B17.18.

laetari oportet quos et amicos amodo possidebo. **128** <u>Praebeo</u> tamen tibi duo
ciliciola ut habeas quibus ualeas operiri." **129** Confusus igitur ad secundum
abiit et similiter eius auxilium postulauit. **130** Cui ille: "Non uacat mihi tecum
subire agonem; **131** curis etenim multis circumdor, modicum tamen usque ad
ostium palatii te sociabo et statim domum reuertar propriis uacans negotiis."

125 *quasi nihil dilexit*: here *quasi* means "almost" ("almost did not love at all/
scarecely loved him"). *Nihil* is **adverbial accusative**, not DO to *dilexit*.
tantum quantum: correlatives ("as much as").
126 *in magno itaque periculo positus . . .* : here *positus* serves as participle of
the verb "to be," i.e., "being in great danger" (cf. G. 7.3.2).
qualiter eum semper dilexerit commemorans: the participle *commemorans*
takes as its DO the **indirect question** with *qualiter* ("how"), a LL question
word = CL *quam*.
127 *quos amicos possidebo*: just as *habeo* in CL can be a **factitive verb** that
means "consider," its synonym *possideo* can be interpreted as "consider" with
quos as DO and *amicos* as **object complement**.
128 *praebeo*: present for future, translate as future tense.
130 *Non uacat mihi*: used impersonally with infinitive *subire* as apparent
subject (A&G 452 and 454), "there is no time for me to . . ."; "I have no time
to. . . ."

124 *iterum (adv.)* furthermore
126 *periculum, i, n.* danger
cito, -are, -aui, -atum summon
qualiter (question word) how much (introduces **indirect question**)
diligo, -ere, -lexi, -lectum like, love
commemoro, -are, -aui, -atum remind, remember
127 *laetor, -ari, -atus sum* rejoice
amodo (adv. LL) from now on
possideo, -ere, -sedi, -sessum have, possess
128 *praebeo, -ere, -bui, -bitum* offer
ciliciolum, ii, n. covering made out of goat skin (here translate as "blanket")
ualeo, -ere, ualui = possum, posse, potui (cf. G. 3.3.1)
operio, -ire, operui, opertum cover
129 *confundo, -ere, -fudi, -fusum* disturb
postulo, -are, -aui, -atum request
130 *uacat (impers.)* time is available to me (+ dat.)
agon, agonis, n. struggle, hardship (LL from Greek *agōn*)
131 *cura, ae, f.* care
circumdo, -are, -aui, -atum surround

modicum, i, n. short distance (LL)
ostium, ii, n. gate
socio, -are, -aui, -atum join, associate
proprius, -a, -um (adj.) own
uaco, -are, -aui, -atum be free to attend to (+ dat)
negotium, ii, n. business, occupation

The third, most neglected friend came to the man's aid in his time of need.

132 Tristis igitur et desperans ad tertium amicum perrexit sibique facie
dimissa dixit: **133** "Non habeo os loquendi ad te quoniam ut debui non
amaui te, sed in tribulatione circumdatus et ab amicis destitutus rogo ut mihi
auxilium feras et mihi ueniam <u>praebeas</u>." **134** Et ille <u>hilari</u> uultu dixit:
135 "Certe amicum carissimum fateor te esse et tui licet modici beneficii non
immemor <u>praecedam</u> te et apud regem interueniam pro te ne in manibus
inimicorum tradat te."

132 *sibi = ei:* refers to the third friend (cf. G. 4.1).
facie dimissa: CL idiom, "with a downcast expression."
133 *non habeo os loquendi ad te:* idiomatic expression, "I do not have the
courage to talk to you."
in tribulatione: CL would have used **ablative of means** without a preposition.
The use of *in* here is a LL feature. (Cf. G. 5.1)
134 *ne in manibus inimicorum tradat te:* biblical language from Daniel 3:32
(the *Vulgata*).
135 *tui licet modici beneficii non immemor: licet* is concessive, functioning as
an adverb with *modici* ("not unmindful of your act of kindness, although a
modest one"). Note the discontinuous noun-phrase *tui . . . beneficii* encircling
the phrase *licet modici.* Cf. G. 6.3.
tui . . . beneficii non immemor: beneficii is genitive with adjective *immemor*
(A&G 349a).
tradat: Maggioni's 2007 edition prints *tradet,* but other manuscripts read
tradat. The subjunctive is needed inside the negative **purpose clause**
introduced by *ne. Tradet* would be an example of ungrammatical Latin (cf.
G. 8).

132 *tristis, -e (adj.)* sad
pergo, -ere, -rexi, -rectum proceed
133 *os, oris, n.* mouth; face (pl. CL)
tribulatio, onis, f. distress
circumdo, -are, -dedi, -datum surround

destituo, -ere, -stitui, -stitutum abandon
auxilium, ii, n. help
uenia, ae, f. forgiveness
praebeo, -ere, -bui, -bitum show, grant
134 *hilaris, -e (adj.)* cheerful
135 *certe (adv.)* certainly
carus, -a, -um (adj.) dear
fateor, -eri, fessus sum admit
modicus, -a, -um (adj.) modest
beneficium, ii, n. act of kindness
immemor, immemoris (adj.) unmindful of (+ gen)
interuenio, -ire, -ueni, -uentum intervene
inimicus, -a, -um (adj.) hostile, (substantive) enemy
trado, -ere, -didi, -ditum hand over

Interpretation of the parable.

136 Primus igitur amicus est diuitiarum possessio pro quibus homo multis periculis subiacet, ueniente uero mortis termino, nihil ex hiis omnibus nisi uiles accepit ad sepeliendum panniculos. **137** Secundus amicus est uxor, filii et parentes qui tantum usque ad monumentum secum pergentes, protinus reuertuntur suis uacantes curis. **138** Tertius amicus est fides, spes et caritas et elemosina et cetera bona opera quae nos, cum de corpore eximus, possunt praecedere et pro nobis apud deum interuenire et ab inimicis daemonibus nos liberare."

136 *homo:* used impersonally.[23] Translate with "one" or "a person."
137 *secum = cum eo:* refers to the generic *homo,* mentioned in 136 (cf. G. 4.1).

136 *diuitiae, arum, f. (pl.)* riches, wealth
possessio, onis, f. possession
periculum, i, n. danger
subiaceo, -ere, -iacui undergo
terminus, i, m. boundary, end point
uilis, -e (adj.) cheap
sepelio, -ire, -iui, -itum bury
panniculum, i, n. shroud (with which the dead are enveloped)
137 *uxor, oris, f.* wife
tantum (adv.) only

---

23. Cf. Elliott (1997) 51 pt. 7.14.1.

monumentum, i, n. grave, tomb
pergo, -ere, -rexi, -rectum proceed
protinus (adv.) immediately
138 *fides, ei, f.* trust
spes, ei, f. hope
caritas, tatis, f. charity, selfless love
elemosina, ae, f. alms, pity (LL from Greek *eleēmosynē*)
opus, eris, n. deed

5.5 BARLAAM'S FIFTH PARABLE: THE KING FOR ONE YEAR

This parable about storing for oneself a treasure in heaven (Matthew 6:19–21) has a distinct Christian overtone, but "it is also found in the earliest version of Barlaam and Josaphat, the Arabic Bilawhar and Būdhāsaf."[24]

139 Hoc insuper addidit dicens: **140** "In quadam magna ciuitate consuetudo fuit quod hominem extraneum et ignotum omni anno in principem eligebant cui omni potestate accepta quidquid uolebat facere licitum erat et sine omni constitutione terram regebat. **141** Illo igitur in omnibus deliciis permanente et semper sibi sic esse existimante, repente ciues in eum insurgebant et per totam ciuitatem nudum trahentes in remotam insulam exulem transmittebant, ubi nec cibum nec uestimentum inueniens fame et frigore urgebatur. **142** Tandem quidam alius sublimatus in regno cum illorum ciuium consuetudinem didicisset, infinitos thesauros ad insulam illam praemisit, ubi post annum in exilium relegatus ceteris fame deficientibus ille immensis deliciis abundabat.

140 *consuetudo fuit quod:* LL **noun result clause** = CL *ut* + subjunctive (cf. G. 3.5.5).
in principem: CL would have used **object complement** with the **factitive verb** *eligo* ("elect"); the use of this prepositional phrase instead is a feature of LL.
cui: **dative of reference** with *licitum erat* ("to whom it had been allowed . . .").
licitum erat: pluperfect tense of the impersonal verb *licet, licuit* with infinitive *facere* as apparent subject (A&G 454).
quidquid uolebat: indefinite relative clause functioning as the DO of *facere* ("to whom it was allowed to do whatever he wanted").
141 *semper sibi sic esse . . . . :* read "*esse*" as "*futurum esse*," used impersonally ("that it will always be so for him"). The man naively thinks that his situation of power is permanent.

---

24. Lopez and McCracken (2014) 224.

140 *extraneus, -a, -um (adj.)* foreign
ignotus, -a, -um (adj.) unknown
princeps, cipis, m. leader, king (CL first citizen, princeps)
eligo, -ere, -legi, -lectum elect
constitutio, onis, f. restriction, condition
141 *existimo, -are, -aui, -atum* think, consider
repente (adv.) suddenly
insurgo, -ere, -rexi, -rectum revolt
nudus, -a, -um (adj.) naked
traho, -ere, traxi, tractum draw, drag
exsul, sulis, m./f. exiled, banished person
cibus, i, m. food
inuenio, -ire, -ueni, -uentum find
fames, is, f. hunger
frigor, is, m. cold
urgeo, -ere, ursi oppress, burden
142 *sublimo, -are, -aui, -atum* raise
regnum, i, n. kingdom
ciuis, is, m./f. citizen
consuetudo, tudinis, f. custom
*disco, -ere, didici,—*learn
infinitus, -a, -um (adj.) boundless
insula, ae, f. island
pr(a)emitto, -ere, -misi, -missum send ahead
exilium, ii, n. exile
relego, -are, -aui, -atum banish
deficio, -ere, -feci, -fectum starve
delicium, ii, n. pleasure, enjoyment
abundo, -are, -aui, -atum have plenty of, abound (in)

Interpretation of the fifth parable.

143 Ciuitas <u>haec</u> mundus iste est; **144** ciues tenebrarum principes qui nos falsa mundi delectatione illiciunt, nobisque insperantibus mors superuenit et in locum tenebrarum demergimur; **145** diuitiarum uero ad <u>aeternum</u> locum <u>praemissio</u> fit manibus egenorum."

144 *ciues tenebrarum principes:* supply *sunt* after *ciues.*
145 *diuitiarum ad <u>aeternum</u> locum <u>praemissio</u> fit manibus egenorum:* the discontinuous noun phrase *diuitiarum . . . praemissio* (cf. G. 6.3) is the subject of *fit* ("happens through the hands of the needy"). The idea is that charity is like sending ahead (*praemissio*) of a treasure for oneself in the eternal abode.

143 mundus, i, m. world
144 tenebra, ae, f. darkness, shadow
falsus, -a, -um (adj.) false, deceptive
delectatio, onis, f. enjoyment
illicio, -ere, -lexi, -lectum allure
insperans, insperantis (adj.) not expecting
mors, mortis, f. death
superuenio, -ire, -ueni, -uentum come upon
demergo, -ere, -mersi, -mersum sink
145 diuitiae, arum, f. (pl.) riches, wealth
aeternus, -a, -um (adj.) eternal
praemissio, onis, f. sending ahead
egenus, -a, -um (adj.) destitute, needy

5.6. BARLAAM'S SIXTH PARABLE: THE RICH YOUTH AND THE POOR MAIDEN. JOSAPHAT RECEIVES BAPTISM

Josaphat wants to follow Barlaam into the desert, but Barlaam puts off the prince with a sixth parable intended to teach him that the firmness of his desire to live in poverty in the desert would be tested. The parable tells a story about a man rejecting a rich bride and falling in love with a girl who praises God with gratitude despite her poverty. She explains to the youth the reason for her contentment. The girl in the parable symbolizes spiritual wisdom ("prudentia") and the youth resembles Josaphat who desires to seek spiritual wisdom by leaving his kingdom behind and embracing the poverty of the monastic way life.

146 Igitur cum Barlaam perfecte filium regis docuisset et ipse eum iam relicto patre sequi uellet, dixit ad eum Barlaam: **147** "Si hoc feceris, cuidam iuueni similis eris qui, cum quandam nobilem nollet desponsare uxorem, ipse renuens aufugit et in quendam locum deueniens uirginem quandam, cuiusdam senis pauperis filiam, laborantem et ore deum laudantem uidit. **148** Ad quam ille: "Quid est quod agis, mulier? **149** Cum enim ita pauper sis, gratiam tamen agis deo ac si magna recepisses ab eo." **150** Ad quem illa: "Sicut parua medicina saepe a magno languore liberat, sic gratiarum actio in paruis donis magnorum efficitur auctrix donorum. **151** Haec tamen quae extrinsecus sunt, nostra non sunt, sed ea quae in nobis sunt et nostra sunt, a deo magna accepi quia me ad suam imaginem fecit, intellectum mihi dedit, ad suam me gloriam uocauit et ianuam regni sui iam mihi aperuit; **152** pro tantis ergo et tam magnis donis ipsum laudare conuenit."

146 *dixit ad eum:* CL would have used the **dative of indirect object** (*dixit ei*).
149 *ac si = tamquam* "as if" (cf. G. 3.5.1).

150 *gratiarum actio:* the CL expression *gratiam/gratias ago* ("thank") becomes a noun phrase here ("the giving of thanks" / "thanksgiving").

in paruis donis: the prepositional phrase has to be taken with *gratiarum actio:* "thanksgiving in the case of small gifts/for small gifts."

auctrix: **subject complement** (i.e., predicate noun) with subject *actio* and **linking verb** *efficitur* = *fit* ("becomes"). Cf G. 7.7.

magnorum . . . donorum: discontinuous noun-phrase (cf. G. 6.3).

151 *ea . . . magna:* a particularly spread-out discontinuous noun-phrase (cf. G. 6.3). *Ea* refers to *dona* and is DO of *accepi* ("I received from God great such gifts which . . .").

152 *conuenit:* the manuscripts print *conueni* here, but only the impersonal verb *conuenit* makes sense. This is another example of ungrammatical Latin (G. 8).

laudare conuenit: the infinitive *laudare* is apparent subject of impersonal verb *conuenit* (A&G 454), i.e., "it is appropriate to praise him."

143 *mundus, i, m.* world
144 *tenebra, ae, f.* darkness, shadow
falsus, -a, -um (adj.) false, deceptive
delectatio, onis, f. enjoyment
illicio, -ere, -lexi, -lectum allure
insperans, insperantis (adj.) not expecting
mors, mortis, f. death
superuenio, -ire, -ueni, -uentum come upon
demergo, -ere, -mersi, -mersum sink
145 *diuitiae, arum, f. (pl.)* riches, wealth
aeternus, -a, -um (adj.) eternal
praemissio, onis, f. sending ahead
egenus, -a, -um (adj.) destitute, needy
146 *perfecte (adv.)* perfectly, thoroughly
doceo, -ere, -cui, doctum teach
147 *desponso, -are, -aui, -atum* betroth (LL) = *despondeo, -ere, -spondi, -sponsum* (CL)
renuo, -ere, -nui, -nutum refuse, decline
deuenio, -ire, -ueni, -uentum arrive
senex, senis, m. old man
laboro, -are, -aui, -atum work
148 *mulier, eris, f.* woman, wife
149 *recipio, -ere, -cepi, -ceptum* receive
150 *languor, oris, m.* illness
libero, -are, -aui, -atum free

gratia, ae, f. favor
actio, onis, f. act, doing
donum, i, n. gift
efficio, -ere, -feci, -fectum make, bring to pass (passive *efficior = fio* become, cf.
   G. 7.7)
auctrix, tricis, f. originator
151 *extrinsecus (adv.)* external, on the outside
accipio, -ere, -cepi, -ceptum take, grasp
imago, inis, f. image, likeness
intellectus, us, m. intellect
ianua, ae, f. door, entrance
aperio, -ire, aperui, apertum uncover, reveal
152 *conuenit (impers.)* it is appropriate, it is right

*The youth asks to marry the girl, but her father sets a condition, in which he
cannot take the girl with him but has to live with the family in their humble
dwelling. The youth agrees to marry the poor girl under these conditions. After
he marries her, he finds out that her father is actually rich.*

153 Videns iuuenis eius prudentiam eam a patre suo in uxorem petiit. **154**
Cui ille: "Filiam meam accipere non uales quia diuitum et nobilium filius es,
ego autem pauper sum." **155** Sed cum ille omnino instaret, ait senex: **156**
"Non possum eam tibi dare ut in domum patris tui ducas eam, cum unica
mihi sit." **157** Et ille: "Apud uos manebo et uobis me in omnibus conformabo."
158 Deponens igitur pretiosum ornamentum habitum senis induit et apud
eum manens ipsam in uxorem accepit. **159** Postquam uero senex diutius eum
probauit, in thalamum eum duxit et immensum pondus diuitiarum, quantum
nunquam uiderat, sibi ostendit et omnia sibi dedit."

153 *a patre suo = a patre eius.* The subject of the sentence is *iuuenis*, but *suo*
refers to the girl, not to the young man (cf. G. 4.1).
petiit = petiuit.
155 *ille*: Maggioni's 2007 edition prints *illo* here, but only *ille* makes
grammatical sense. This is another example of ungrammatical Latin (cf. G. 8).
159 *sibi = ei*: refers to the youth (cf. G. 4.1).

153 *prudentia, ae, f.* wisdom
154 *diues, diuitis (adj.)* rich
nobilis, -e (adj.) noble
pauper, -is (adj.) poor
155 *omnino (adv.)* completely, thoroughly

insto, -are, -stiti insist
senex, senis, m. old man
156 *duco, -ere, duxi, ductum* lead
unicus, -a, -um (adj.) only, single
157 *apud (prep + acc)* near (*apud vos* "in your house")
maneo, -ere, mansi stay, remain
conformo, -are, -aui, -atum adjust oneself to (+ dat)
158 *depono, -ere, -posui, -positum* put away
pretiosus, -a, -um (adj.) expensive, costly
ornamentum, i, n. ornament, trappings
induo, -ere, -dui, -dutum put on
159 *diutius (comparative adv. of diu)* for a longer time
probo, -are, -aui, -atum test
thalamus, i, m. bedroom, marriage
immensus, -a, -um (adj.) huge
pondus, ponderis, n. mass
ostendo, -ere, -di, ostensum show

Using scriptural language from the letters of St. Paul (Rom 7:22; 2 Cor. 4:16; and 1 Peter 3:4) Barlaam explains how he calculates the years of his life. He counts only those years when he was aware of his inward man and he does not count the years when he was dead to his inward man. Josaphat reiterates his aspiration to leave the palace and follow him. Barlaam dissuades him again but baptizes the prince and returns to the desert.

160 Dixit autem Iosaphat: **161** "Conuenienter me ista tangit narratio et a te hoc dictum esse de me existimo, sed dic mihi, pater, quot annorum es et ubi conuersaris, quia a te nunquam uolo separari." **162** Et ille: "Annorum sum XLV in desertis terrae Sennaar degens." **163** Ad quem Iosaphat: "Amplius mihi, pater, appares LXX annorum." **164** Et ille: "Si a natiuitate mea omnes annos meos quaeris discere, bene eos existimasti, sed nullo modo a me in mensura uitae computantur quotquot in uanitate mundi expensi sunt; **165** tunc enim in interiori homine mortuus eram et annos mortis nunquam uitae nominabo." **166** Cum igitur Iosaphat eum in desertum sequi uellet dixit Barlaam: **167** "Si hoc feceris et tuo consortio carebo et persecutionis fratribus meis auctor existam, sed cum oportunum tempus uideris, ad me uenies." **168** Barlaam igitur filium regis baptizans et in fide optime instruens eum osculatus est et ad locum suum reuersus est.

163 *Amplius LXX annorum: amplius* is **subject complement** (i.e., predicate adjective) with subject *tu* and **linking verb** *appares* = CL *uideris* (cf. G. 7.7).

LXX annorum is genitive of quality expressing measure (A&G 345b) after the comparative *amplius* without *quam* (A&G 407c). Translate as "you seem to me more than 70 years old."

164 *quaeris discere:* LL infinitive of the goal (cf. G. 3.3.2), "you seek to learn."

165 *in interiori homine:* language from St. Paul's Letter 2 to Corinthians 4:16, Romans 7:22, and 1 Peter 3:4.

167 *et tuo consortio carebo et persecutionis fratribus meis auctor existam:* Barlaam knows that if he takes Josaphat with him into the desert, the king will find and kill him, and so Josaphat will be separated from him. In addition, the king will unleash his wrath for the abduction of his son on the monks and will intensify their persecutions. This is why Barlaam would be the root-cause (*auctor*) of these persecutions.

persecutionis *fratribus meis* auctor: another discontinuous noun-phrase (cf. G. 6.3).

161 *conuenienter (adv.)* suitably
tango, -ere, tetigi, tactum strike, touch
existimo, -are, -aui, -atum think, consider
conuersor, -ari, -atus sum live
separo, -are, -aui, -atum separate
162 *Senaar (indecl. place name)* the land between Tigris and Euphrates, known later as Chaldea or Babylonia.[25]
dego, -ere, -egi spend time
163 *amplius (comparative adverb from amplus, -a, -um)* = *plus* in CL
164 *existimo, -are, -aui, -atum* estimate, think, consider
mensura, ae, f. measurement
computo, -are, -aui, -atum calculate
quotquot (indecl adj.) however many
uanitas, tatis, f. emptiness, vanity
expendo, -ere, -pendi, -pensum spend
167 *consortio, onis, n.* fellowship, community
careo, -ere, -ui, -itum lack
auctor, is, m. originator, agent
ex(s)isto, -ere, -(s)titi, -stitum = *sum* (LL cf. G. 7.3.1)
168 *instruo, -ere, -struxi, -structum* instruct
osculor, -ari, -atus sum kiss

---

25. Woodward and Mattingly (1997) 624 (index).

Part 6: King Avenir's Effort to Bring the Prince Back to Idol-Worship with the Help of Fake Barlaam

The king learns about his son's conversion to Christianity and baptism. He is in great distress. One of his friends, Arachis, devises a plot to turn the prince away from Christianity through deception. He requests to be put in charge of an army and to be sent on a mission of capturing Barlaam. If the mission fails, the army will claim to have captured Barlaam and will return with a pagan hermit (Nachor) who looks like Barlaam.

Since this is a compressed version of the story, Jacobus de Voragine did not include the details of Arachis's plan described in chapter 193 of the long version. The plan of Arachis consists of the following: the king should try to capture Barlaam; if he cannot do that, he should pretend to have captured Barlaam, but in reality the pagan hermit Nachor, who is Arachis's teacher and is similar in appearance to Barlaam, will disguise himself as Barlaam. The king should announce that Barlaam was captured and should stage a theological debate between fake Barlaam and the king's learned debaters (rhetors). The desired outcome of the debate is this: Nachor would let himself be defeated; the defeat would publicly discredit Barlaam and his Christianity; as a result, Prince Josaphat, disappointed with Barlaam, would return to idolatry.[26]

Josaphat through divine revelation finds out that the capturing of Barlaam is a ruse.

169 Postquam autem rex filium christianum factum audiuit, in dolore nimio positus est. **170** Quem quidam amicus suus nomine Arachis consolans ait: **171** "Cognosco, rex, senem quendam heremitam, qui de nostra secta est, qui per omnia Barlaam similis est; **172** hic igitur Barlaam se simulans primo christianorum fidem defendet, deinde se superari permittet et omnia <u>quae</u> docuerat reuocabit et sic filius regis ad nos redibit." **173** Assumpto igitur <u>praedicto</u> principe magno exercitu ad <u>quaerendum</u> Barlaam iuit et heremitam illum capiens se Barlaam cepisse dixit. **174** Quod filius regis audiens, captum scilicet magistrum amare fleuit, sed postmodum per dei reuelationem hunc non esse cognouit.

169 *in dolore nimio positus est:* translate *positus est* as a form of *sum* (cf. G. 7.3.2).
170 *Quem:* **connecting relative**, DO of *consolans*, refers to the king.

---

26. Cruz Palma (2001) 346.

amicus suus = amicus eius (cf. G. 4.1): *eius* refers to the king.
171 *Barlaam* (indeclinable) is **dative with adjective** *similis* ("similar to").
172 *Barlaam se simulans:* supply *esse* for this **indirect statement**, governed
by *simulans* "pretending that he was Barlaam." *Barlaam* (indeclinable) is the
accusative subject of the **indirect statement**.
173 *praedicto principe:* an instance of ungrammatical Latin (cf. G. 8). It is
ablative of agent from which the preposition *a* was left out. The **ablative
absolute** should read (crude translation): "With a great army having been
received by the nobleman (i.e., Arachis, the king's friend)."
praedicto = definite article "the"; do not translate literally as "aforementioned"
(cf. G. 7.1).
174 *quod:* **connecting relative**, refers to the false claim that Barlaam was
captured.
captum scilicet magistrum: supply *esse* for an **indirect statement** that
functions as appositive to *quod* ("hearing this, namely that his teacher had
been captured").
amare fleuit: note that *amare* is adverb with *fleuit.*
hunc non esse: supply *suum magistrum. Hunc* refers to captured Nachor, i.e.,
fake Barlaam.

169 *dolor, is, m.* pain, sorrow
nimius, -a, -um (adj.) excessive
170 *Arachis, is, m.* personal name
171 *senex, senis (adj.)* old
secta, ae, f. sect, religion
172 *simulo, -are, -aui, -atum* pretend
supero, -are, -aui, -atum defeat
redeo, -ire, -ii, -itum return
173 *assumo, -ere, -sumpsi, -sumptum* receive
174 *scilicet (adv.)* namely, that is
amare (adv.) bitterly
fleo, -ere, -eui, -etum cry for, weep
postmodum (adv.) after a while
reuelatio, onis, f. revelation

King Avenir confronts Josaphat about his conversion.

175 Ingressus igitur pater ad filium ait: **176** "Fili mi, in tristitia magna me
posuisti et meam canitiem inhonorasti et lumen oculorum meorum abstulisti;
177 quare, fili, hoc fecisti et deorum meorum cultum reliquisti ?"**178** Cui ille:
"Tenebras, pater, fugi, ad lumen cucurri, errorem deserui et ueritatem agnoui,

noli autem frustra laborare, quoniam nunquam a Christo me posses reuocare. Sicut enim tibi impossibile est altitudinem <u>caeli</u> manu tangere aut maximum siccare pelagus, sic et istud esse cognosce."

178 *noli laborare:* **negative command** (CL) "do not try."
178 *quoniam* + subjunctive is LL use (A&G 540 note 1 and 540.2a). *Quoniam* in CL introduces a reason given on the authority of the writer or speaker and therefore always takes the indicative.
Sicut enim tibi impossibile est . . . sic et istud esse cognosce: the pronoun *istud* refers to the attempt to divert Josaphat from becoming a Christian monk.
Et = etiam: (cf. G. 7.9) "Just as . . . so also recognize that *even* this (i.e., to recall me from Christ) is (impossible)."
et istud esse cognosce: supply *impossibile* with *esse.* The parallelism of *sicut . . . sic* makes this **gapping** (ellipsis) possible to detect.

175 *ingredior, -gredi, -gressus sum* enter
176 *tristitia, ae, f.* sadness, sorrow
canities, ei, f. old age
inhonoro, -are, -aui, -atum dishonor
aufero, -ferre, abstuli, ablatum take away
177 *quare (adv.)* why
cultus, us, m. worship
178 *curro, -ere, cucurri, cursum* run
frustra (adv.) in vain
nunquam = numquam (CL)
impossibilis, -e (adj.) impossible
altitudo, inis, f. height
sicco, -are, -aui, -atum dry out, make dry
pelagus, i, n. sea

Josaphat defends his faith before his angry father who threatens to punish him.

179 Tunc rex ait: **180** "Et quis horum mihi est auctor malorum, nisi ego, qui tam magnifica tibi feci, <u>quae</u> nunquam aliquis patrum fecit filio suo? **181** Quapropter prauitas <u>tuae</u> uoluntatis et contentio effrenata aduersus caput meum te insanire fecit. **182** Merito astrologi in natiuitate tua dixerunt te arrogantem et parentibus <u>inoboedientem</u> futurum. **183** Nunc uero nisi mihi acquieueris a mea discedes filiatione et pro patre inimicus effectus illa tibi faciam <u>quae</u> nec hostibus adhuc feci." **184** Cui Iosaphat: "Cur, rex, tristaris quia bonorum particeps sum effectus? **185** Quis unquam pater in filii sui prosperitate tristis apparuit? **186** Non ergo iam patrem uocabo te sed, si mihi aduersaberis, sicut a serpente fugiam a te."

180 *tam magnifica tibi feci:* "I did such great things for you."
aliquis patrum: **partitive genitive** ("any of the fathers," i.e., "any father").
181 *te insanire fecit:* cf. G. 3.1.
182 *futurum:* supply *esse* for the infinitive verb of the **indirect statement** after *dixerunt*.
184 *Cur tristaris quia:* LL **indirect statement** ("Why are you sad that . . ."). Cf. G. 3.2.
185 *tristis:* **subject complement** (i.e., predicate adjective) with subject *pater* and **linking verb** *apparuit* = CL *uisus est.* Cf. G. 7.7.

180 *magnificus, -a, -um (adj.)* great
nunquam (adv.) never
181 *quapropter (adv.)* therefore
prauitas, tatis, f. wickedness
uoluntas, tatis, f. will, goal
contentio, onis, f. confrontational attitude
effrenatus, -a, -um (adj.) mad, unrestrained
insanio, -ire, -iui, -itum be mad
182 *merito (adv.)* rightly
astrologus, i, m. astrologer
arrogo, -are, -aui, -atum assume, question
inoboediens, inoboedientis (adj.) disobedient
183 *acquiesco, -ere, -eui, -etum* submit, make peace with
discedo, -ere, -cessi leave
filiatio, onis, f. sonship, descent-from-father (LL)
adhuc (adv.) so far, again
184 *tristor, -ari, -atus sum* be sad, grieve
particeps, participis (subst. adj.) partaker, recipient
efficio, -ere, -feci, -fectum make, bring to pass (passive *efficior = fio* become, cf. G. 7.7)
185 *apparet = CL uidetur* seems (cf. G. 7.7)
186 *aduersor, -ari, -atus sum* oppose, resist

The king switches strategy and gently demands obedience from his son.

187 Rex igitur ab eo cum ira discedens Arachi amico notam fecit filii duritiam. **188** Qui sibi consuluit ut non asperis uerbis cum eo uteretur, quia

blandis et lenibus puer melius traheretur. **189** Sequenti igitur die rex ad filium
uenit et circumplectens osculabatur eum dicens: **190** "Fili dulcissime, honora
canitiem patris tui, uerere, fili, patrem tuum; **191** an nescis quale bonum est
patri obedire et eum <u>laetificare</u>, sicut e contra malum est ipsum²⁷ exacerbare?
192 Quotquot enim fecerunt, male perierunt."

187 *notam fecit filii duritiam:* "the king . . . explained (made known) to his
friend Arachis the stubbornness of his son." For the LL compound *notam
facere,* cf. G. 2.2.1.
188 *Qui:* **connecting relative**, refers to Arachis, the king's friend.
sibi = ei: refers to the king.
blandis et lenibus: supply *uerbis.*
traheretur: from *traho* ("drag"). Here means literally, "be pulled along," i.e., "be
brought along."
190 *uerere:* deponent imperative from *uereor.*
fili: vocative of *filius.*
191 *e contra* ("to the contrary"): for the LL combination of prepositions to
form an adverb, cf. G. 5.2.
192 *quotquot enim (id) fecerunt:* "however many people did this."

187 *Arachis, is, m.* Arachis (personal name)
nosco, -ere, noui, notum know, become acquainted with
duritia, ae, f. insensibility, harshness
188 *asper, -a, -um (adj.)* rough, unrefined
blandus, -a, -um (adj.) pleasant, alluring
189 *circumplecto, -ere, -plexi, -plectum* encompass
osculor, -ari, -atus sum kiss, embrace
190 *honoro, -are, -aui, -atum* honor
canities, ei, f. gray hair
uereor, -eri, ueritus sum respect
191 *qualis, -e (adj.)* what kind/sort (of)
laetifico, -are, -aui, -atum delight, gladden
192 *quotquot + indefinite relative clause* however many, as many as
pereo, -ire, -ii perish

---

27. Maggioni's (2007) edition reads *ipsos,* a corrupt reading.

Part 7. The Debate between Fake Barlaam (Nachor) and the Pagan Orators

Josaphat and the king agree on the terms of a debate between fake Barlaam and a group of defenders of the pagan faith. The loser in the debate will have to join the faith of the winner.

193 Cui Iosaphat: "Tempus amandi et tempus odiendi, tempus pacis et tempus belli; **194** nullo enim modo auertentibus nos a deo <u>oboedire</u> debemus, siue sit pater, siue sit mater." **195** Videns igitur pater eius constantiam ait: **196** "Ex quo tuam uideo pertinaciam nec mihi obedire uis, saltem ueni et ambo pariter ueritati credamus. **197** Barlaam enim, qui te seduxit a me uinctus tenetur; **198** nostri igitur et uestri cum Barlaam conueniant et <u>praeconem</u> mittam ut omnes Galilei sine timore ueniant, et disputatione incepta, si uester Barlaam obtinuerit, uobis credemus; **199** si autem nostri, nobis consentietis."

193 *tempus (est) amandi. . .* : approximate quote from *Ecclesiastes* 3.1–8.
194 *auertentibus nos a deo:* substantively used participle in the dative plural ("the ones turning us away from God") with *oboedire debemus*. It forms its own clause with DO *nos* and **ablative of separation** *a deo*. Cf. G. 3.6.
196 *ex quo = CL quod, quia, quoniam* ("since"), introducing a **causal clause**. Cf. G. 3.5.3.
ueni: imperative 2nd sg. *Et* connects *ueni* to the **jussive subjunctive** *credamus*.
198 *nostri igitur et uestri cum Barlaam:* the nominative plural pronominal adjectives *nostri* and *vestri* are used substantively with implied *rhetores*. Take *cum Barlaam* closely with *uestri*. The public debate will take place between two teams: "our orators and your orators with (fake) Barlaam." In reality, as we shall see later, fake Barlaam, i.e., Nachor will debate the king's orators alone. The long Latin version says that a certain Barachias was the only Christian who had the courage to join the team defending Christianity.[28] He is mentioned in chapter 279 as the person to whom Josaphat leaves his kingdom when he becomes a monk.

194 *auerto, -ere, -uerti, -uersum* turn away
oboedio, -ire, -iui, -itum obey, listen (+ dat)
195 *constantia, ae, f.* firmness, perserverance
196 *pertinacia, ae, f.* stubbornness, perseverance
saltem (adv.) at least
197 *uincio, -ire, uinxi, uinctum* bind

---

28. Cruz-Palma (2001) 234.

198 *praeco, onis, m.* herald, crier
Galilei (nom. pl. m.) Galileans, refers to the Christians (LL)
obtineo, -ere, -tinui, -tentum prevail, succeed
199 *consentio, -ire, -sensi, -sensum* agree with

Jacobus's abridged version gives the name of fake Barlaam as Nachor for the first time here. Josaphat tells Nachor that if he does not defend the Christian cause well, he will punish him severely. Now Nachor finds himself in a double bind. If he is the loser in the debate (according to his agreement with King Avenir), Josaphat will punish him. If he is the winner, King Avenir will punish him and he will have betrayed his pagan faith.

200 Quod cum regis filio placuisset et illi cum simulato Barlaam ordinassent quomodo prius debebat simulare se fidem christianorum defendere et postea se promittere superari, omnes insimul conuenerunt. **201** Conuersus igitur Iosaphat ad Nachor dixit: **202** "Nosti, o Barlaam, qualiter me docuisti. **203** Si igitur fidem quam me docuisti defenderis, in doctrina tua usque ad finem <u>uitae</u> permanebo. **204** Si autem superatus fueris, statim in te meam contumeliam uindicabo et cor tuum et linguam manibus extrahens canibus dabo ne alii amplius <u>praesumant</u> filios regum in errorem mittere."

200 There are two *cum*-clauses in this sentence, connected with *et*. *Illi* is the subject of the second *cum*-clause. The referent is the king and his courtiers who are arranging the rigged debate: fake Barlaam, i.e., Nachor, at first has to pretend that he is defending the Christian faith and then he has to let himself be defeated.
quomodo: introduces **indirect question** after *ordinassent* ("They prescribed how . . ."). The use of the indicative in this **indirect question** is a LL feature (cf. G. 3.4). CL would have used the subjunctive.
ordinassent: syncopated form of *ordinauissent*.
debebat simulare: LL compound future with *debeo* + infinitive (cf. G. 2.3.1).
insimul: LL compound adverb (cf. G. 5.2).
202 *nosti:* syncopated form of *nouisti* from *nosco*.

200 *simulo, -are, -aui, -atum* pretend, imitate
ordino, -are, -aui, -atum prescribe
quomodo (question word) how
supero, -are, -aui, -atum overcome, defeat
insimul (adv.) at the same time
202 *qualiter (question word)* how
203 *usque (adv.)* all the way

204 *contumelia, ae, f.* insult, injury
cor, cordis, n. heart
extraho, -ere, -traxi, -tractum remove
praesumo, -ere, -sumpsi, -sumptum dare (LL) = *audeo* (CL) (cf. G. 3.3.1)

Scared by Josaphat's threats, Nachor decides to defend Christianity properly. The debate begins and the king's debaters (rhetors) challenge fake Barlaam, i.e., Nachor, to defend his faith.

205 His auditis Nachor tristis et pauidus uehementer effectus est, uidens se ipsum in foueam quam fecit decidisse et laqueo suo comprehensum esse. **206** Animaduertens igitur cognouit melius esse filio regis adhaerere ut periculum mortis euadere posset. **207** Rex autem sibi palam dixerat ut fidem suam sine timore defenderet. **208** Unus ergo rhetorum surgens dixit: **209** "Tu es Barlaam qui filium regis seduxisti?" **210** Et ille: "Ego sum Barlaam qui filium regis non in errorem misi, sed ab errore liberaui." **211** Et rhetor: "Cum eximii et mirabiles uiri deos nostros adorauerunt, quomodo tu aduersus eos audes insurgere?"

205 *effectus est* is a **linking verb** with *tristis* as its **subject complement** (i.e., predicate adjective) and *Nachor* as subject. Cf. G. 7.7.
207 *sibi* = *ei:* refers to Nachor (cf. G. 4.1).
dixerat here is a command verb and takes **indirect command**. *Dico* in CL can only take **indirect statement**. The construction used here is similar to English "I told him to do it."

205 *tristis, -e (adj.)* sad
pauidus, -a, -um (adj.) trembling, terrified
uehementer (adv.) exceedingly, violently
fouea, ae, f. snare, pit
decido, -ere, -cidi fall down
laqueus, i, m. trap
206 *animaduerto, -ere, -uerti, -uersum* pay attention to, observe
adhaereo, -ere, -haesi, -haesum stick to
207 *palam (adv.)* openly
208 *rhetor, oris, m.* debater, teacher of rhetoric, orator (from Greek *rhētōr*)
209 *seduco, -ere, -duxi, -ductum* lead astray
211 *eximius, -a, -um (adj.)* special, remarkable
adoro, -are, -aui, -atum worship, honor
aduersus (prep + acc) against
insurgo, -ere, -rexi, -rectum rise up

This section is a greatly compressed version of the "Apology of Aristides," the
full text of which is eight pages in the Greek version and its Latin translation
(Cf. Introd. 1.2.4 and 1.2.5). The defense ("apologia" in Greek) is an important
historical source dated to 125 CE, believed lost for a long time. It is called
"Apology of Aristides" because the philosopher Aristides, a convert to
Christianity, delivered it to Emperor Hadrian in Athens. Aristides described in
detail many of the beliefs and practices of the Chaldeans, ancient Greeks, and the
Egyptians in the process of showing how Christianity was ethically superior to
those three pagan religions. Emperor Hadrian was so impressed with Aristides's
defense that he issued an order stopping the persecution of Christians without
proper investigation and trial.[29]

The circumstances in which Aristides delivered his defence (apologia) to
Hadrian bear some similarities to the circumstances in which fake Barlaam
(Nachor) defends Christianity to King Avenir. The person who inserted the
"Apology of Aristides" into the body of this legend was a master interpolator. The
double identity of Aristides, who continued to wear the philosopher's garb after
his conversion,[30] *is similar to the double identity of the pagan astrologer and*
magus Nachor disguised as the Christian hermit Barlaam.

Jacobus de Voragine compressed the "Apology of Aristides" into six sentences
(213–19). In the process, he made a crude factual mistake in the summary of
the ancient Greek myths. He incorrectly states that Saturn (Chronos in Greek)
devoured his sons and cut off his own genitals (215). The longer Latin version,
faithfully following the original Greek, renders the myth correctly, i.e., Jupiter
cut off the genitals of his father Saturn,[31] *threw them into the sea and from them*
Venus was born. Aphrodite is the Greek name for Venus. The name of Aphrodite
was believed to derive its etymology from the foam (Greek "aphros") formed
when the genitals of Saturn fell into the sea.

In other Greek versions of the myth, Chronos cut off the genitals of his father
Uranos when he was lying with his wife Gaia (Earth).

212 Et ille respondens ait: **213** "Chaldei, <u>Graeci</u> et <u>Aegyptii</u> errantes creaturas
deos esse dixerunt. **214** Nam Chaldei elementa deos arbitrati sunt, cum
creata sint ad utilitatem hominum ut eorum dominationi subiaceant et
multis passionibus corrumpantur. **215** <u>Graeci</u> quoque nefandos homines
deos esse putant, sicut Saturnum, quem aiunt filios suos comedisse et

---

29. For the discovery of the *Apology of Aristides*, cf. Lopez and McCracken (2014) 134–36.

30. Lopez and McCracken (2014) 134.

31. *Inducitur enim ab eis ante omnes deos Saturnus, et huic sacrificant filios suos, qui genuit multos*
pueros de Rea et insaniens comedit filios suos. Aiunt autem Iouem absidisse sibi uirilia et proiecisse
in mare, unde Venus fabulose dicitur fuisse nata (chapter 245, p. 404 in de la Cruz Palma, Óscar
(2001)).

uirilia sibi abscidisse et in mare proiecisse et Venerem inde natam fuisse, a filio quoque suo Ioue alligatum et in Tartarum proiectum esse. **216** Iupiter quoque rex aliorum deorum esse describitur quem tamen in animalia <u>saepe</u> transformatum dicunt ut adulteria committeret. **217** Venerem quoque deam adulteram esse dicunt, nam aliquando habuit <u>moechum</u> Martem, aliquando Adonidem. **218** <u>Aegyptii</u> autem animalia coluerunt scilicet ouem, uitulum, porcum et huiusmodi. **219** Christiani autem filium altissimi colunt qui de <u>caelo</u> descendit et carnem assumpsit."

214 *elementa deos arbitrati sunt:* here *arbitror* is a **factitive verb** with *elementa* as its DO and *deos* as **object complement**.
cum creata sint: the *cum*-clause is **concessive**.
ut eorum dominationi subiaceant et multis passionibus corrumpantur: take *ut* as **result clause** and the Chaldeans as subject of both verbs in the clause.
217 *aliquando . . . aliquando:* at one time . . . at another time.
Mars, the god of war was Venus's lover. Venus's husband Vulcan (Hephaestus) installed a chain-trap on the lovers' bed and summoned all the gods to witness his wife's infidelity. Homer reports this humorous episode in the *Odyssey* (8.266–366).
Adonis was a young vegetation god with whom Venus fell in love (Ovid, *Metamorphoses* X.503–741) and preferred him even to heaven. Despite her warnings about the dangers from the wild beasts of the forest, Adonis paid no heed to her warnings and was killed by a wild boar. He died in the hands of Venus who transformed his blood into the flower anemone.
219 *altissimi:* genitive singular of the **substantive adjective** for God ("the highest one").

213 *Chaldeus, -a, -um (adj.)* Chaldean (person from Babylon)
creatura, ae, f. creature
214 *elementum, i, n.* natural element
subiaceo, -ere, -iacui be subject to
passio, onis, f. passion
corrumpo, -ere, -rupi, -ruptum corrupt, entice
215 *Graecus, -a, -um (adj.)* Greek, of the Greeks
nefandus, -a, -um (adj.) impious, wicked
sicut (adv.) just as, like
comedo, -ere, -edi, -essum eat
uirilis, -e (adj.) manly, masculine; (subst.) genitals
abscido, -ere, -cidi, ascisum cut off, amputate
proicio, -ere, -ieci, -iectum throw away
Venus, eris, f. Venus, the goddess of love (from Greek mythology)

nascor, nasci, natus sum be born
Iuppiter, Iouis, m. Jupiter
alligo, -are, -aui, -atum bind
Tartarus, i, m. Underworld
216 *adulterium, ii, n.* adultery
217 *adultera, ae, f.* adulteress
aliquando (adv.) at some point in time
moechus, i, m. lover
Adonis, Adonidis, m. one of Venus's lovers in mythology
218 *colo, -ere, -ui, cultum* worship, honor
scilicet (adv.) namely, that is
ouis, is, m./f. sheep
uitulus, i, m. male calf
huiusmodi (LL indecl. pronoun) such things (cf. G. 4.4)
219 *assumo, -ere, -sumpsi, -sumptum* receive

*Nachor defends the Christian faith too convincingly, failing to honor his promise
to discredit Christianity and thus bring the prince back to idolatry. The king is
furious at Nachor's betrayal and dismisses the gathering. Josaphat knows that
Nachor is not actually Barlaam but asks his father to let "Barlaam" remain
with him for the night, so that the two can discuss their next moves. The king
agrees because he still hopes that Nachor will honor his pledge to divert Josaphat
from Christianity. However, it is Josaphat who converts Nachor and, in the end,
Nachor is baptized and becomes a Christian hermit.*

220 Coepit igitur Nachor fidem christianorum euidenter defendere et
rationibus communire, ita quod rhetores illi muti effecti nihil omnino
respondere sciuerunt. **221** Iosaphat igitur uehementer exultabat, eo quod
dominus per inimicum ueritatis ueritatem defendisset, rex autem furore
nimio repletus est. **222** Iussit igitur consilium dissolui quasi de his sequenti
die denuo tractaturus, dixitque Iosaphat patri: **223** "Aut magistrum meum
permitte mecum hac nocte manere ut simul de responsionibus fiendis
crastino conferamus et tu tuos tecum assumas et cum eis conferas aut tuis
mecum permissis, accipe meum. **224** Alioquin non iustitiam sed uiolentiam
exercebis." **225** Quapropter Nachor sibi concessit spem adhuc habens quod
eum seduceret. **226** Cum igitur filius regis cum Nachor domum redisset, dixit
ei Iosaphat: **227** "Ne putes me ignorare quis sis; **228** scio te non esse Barlaam,
sed Nachor astrologum." **229** Incipiensque Iosaphat uiam salutis ei predicauit
et ad fidem conuertens mane ad heremum misit ubi baptismum suscipiens
heremiticam uitam duxit.

220 *ita quod + indicative* = CL *ut* + subjunctive expressing **result clause** (cf G. 3.5.4). "Nachor began to openly defend the faith of the Christians and to support it with arguments in such a way that . . . ."
respondere sciuerunt: for *scio* + **complementary infinitive** = *possum* (cf. G. 3.3.1).
221 *eo quod . . . :* *eo* is **ablative of cause**, setting up a causal *quod* ("for this reason, because . . ."); *dominus,* i.e. *deus.*
223 *de responsionibus fiendis crastino:* take *crastino* as an adverb with the **gerundive** *fiendis* "concerning the responses about to be made tomorrow." This use of the **gerundive** is rare in CL. For the LL gerundive without the connotation of obligation or necessity, cf. G. 2.5.
tuis mecum permissis: **ablative absolute**, i.e., "with your people having been allowed (to stay) with me."
meum: "my guy," i.e., fake Barlaam. Josaphat offers his father two options 1) either to let fake Barlaam stay with him while the king takes the orators with him or 2) the king should take fake Barlaam with him and leave the orators with Josaphat. The king chooses the first option, miscalculating again.
225 *Quapropter Nachor sibi concessit:* the narrative here is compressed and can be understood by consulting the longer version. The subject of *concessit* is the king; *sibi* refers to Josaphat; Nachor (indeclinable) is the DO of *concessit* ("Therefore, the king yielded Nachor to him, i.e., to Josaphat").
spem habens = *sperans* (cf. G. 2.2.1).
spem habens quod: LL **indirect statement** "hoping that" (cf. G. 3.2). Nachor is the subject of the *quod*-clause.
seduceret has a future sense = CL *Nachor (Acc sg) eum (Iosaphat) seducturum esse.* The king is hoping that Nachor will lead Josaphat astray, i.e., convert him back to idolatry.
227 *Ne putes:* **jussive subjunctive** in a prohibition ("Don't think that . . .").

220 *euidenter (adv.)* openly
defendo, -ere, -di, -fensum defend, protect
ratio, onis, f. argument
communio, -ire, -iui, -itum fortify thoroughly, secure
rhetor, oris, m. debater, teacher of rhetoric, orator (from Greek *rhētōr*)
mutus, -a, -um (adj.) speechless
omnino (adv.) at all, altogether
221 *exsulto, -are, -aui, -atum* rejoice, exult
furor, oris, m. rage, fury
repleo, -ere, -eui, -etum fill up, replenish
222 *denuo (adv.)* again, a second time
223 *responsio, onis, f.* answer, reply

crastino = *cras (adv.)* tomorrow
confero, -ferre, -tuli, collatum consult together, confer
224 *alioqui(n) (adv.)* otherwise
exerceo, -ere, -cui, -citum exercise, practice
225 *quapropter (adv.)* therefore
concedo, -ere, -cessi, -cessum yield
seduco, -ere, -duxi, -ductum lead astray
226 *redeo, -ire, -ii, -itum* go back, come back
227 *ignoro, -are, -aui, -atum* not know, be ignorant
229 *salus, salutis, f.* salvation, safety
praedico, -are, -aui, -atum predict, foretell (LL); announce, proclaim (CL)
conuerto, -ere, -uerti, -uersum direct to/towards
heremus, i, m. wilderness, desert (LL from Greek *erēmos*)
heremiticus, -a, -um (adj.) heremitical (LL)

Part 8: The Prince in the Cave Allegory and Josaphat's Sexual Temptations

After the scheme with fake Barlaam fails, the magus Theodas promises to help the king bring his son back to idolatry. He advises King Avenir to draw the prince away from ascetic piety by surrounding him with attractive women.

230 Magus autem quidam nomine Theodas <u>haec quae</u> gerebantur audiens ad regem uenit et quod filium suum ad leges patrias redire faceret promisit. **231** Cui rex: "Si hoc feceris statuam auream tibi erigam et ipsi sicut diis sacrificium offeram." **232** Et ille: "A filio tuo cunctos remoue et mulieres decoras et ornatas introduci <u>praecipe</u> ut semper cum eo sint et ministrent ei et conuersentur et morentur cum eo. **233** Ego autem unum de spiritibus meis ad eum dirigam qui eum ad libidinem inflammabit. **234** Nihil enim iuuenes sic potest seducere sicut facies mulierum.

230 The sentence contains both a LL **indirect statement** with *quod* and a LL infinitive for result clause with *facio* (cf. G. 3.1 and 3.2). *Facio* here means "compel."
231 *ipsi* (dat. sg.) = *tibi*.
232 *praecipe*: imperative with **objective infinitive** *introduci* and its accusative subject *mulieres* ("order beautiful and well-dressed women to be led in").
ut: **purpose clause.**

231 *statua, ae, f.* statue, image

aureus, -a, -um (adj.) golden
erigo, -ere, -rexi, -rectum erect, set up
232 *cunctus, -a, -um (adj.)* all as a group
mulier, eris, f. woman
decorus, -a, -um (adj.) beautiful, graceful
ornatus, -a, -um (adj.) well-dressed
introduco, -ere, -duxi, -ductum lead in
praecipio, -ere, -cepi, -ceptum order
ministro, -are, -aui, -atum serve, wait
conuerso, -are, -aui, -atum have dealings
moror, -ari, -atus sum stay, delay
233 *dirigo, -ere, -rexi, -rectum* direct, arrange
libido, inis, f. lust
inflammo, -are, -aui, -atum inflame
234 *facies, ei, f.* face

*To convince the king of the effectiveness of his strategy, Theodas tells him a
fable about a king and his son who, just like Josaphat, was raised in isolation.
The prince in the fable grew up in a dark cave because he was fated to lose his
eyesight if he were to see the sun before he turned ten. Since the prince had no
permission to see either the sun or fire, he could not see anything and could
not learn the names of things. He started to familiarize himself with the world
around him after he turned ten.*

235 Rex enim quidam cum filium uix habuisset dixerunt peritissimi medici
quod si infra annos decem solem uel lunam uiderit lumine oculorum
priuabitur. **236** Rex igitur in quādam petrā speluncā excisā filium ibi usque
ad annos decem manere fecit. **237** Quibus finitis iussit rex ut omnium
rerum genera ante eum adducerentur ut omnium nomina et notitiam posset
habere. **238** Adductis igitur ante eum auro et argento, lapidibus pretiosis,
uestibus splendidis, equis regalibus et omnium rerum generibus, cum de
uniuscuiusque rei nomine interrogaret, ministri omnium sibi nomina
indicabant.

235 *Rex . . . quidam*: subject of the *cum*-clause, even though it is outside the
clause.
uiderit: future perfect because of the simple future *priuabitur* in the main
clause. The subject is the king's son.
quod: cf. G. 3.2.
236 *in quādam petrā speluncā excisā*: the word order of this **ablative absolute**
is not classical. CL would have placed the prepositional phrase between *petrā*

and *excisā.*

usque ad annos decem: the Greek version of the legend says "twelve years,"
which fits better with the rest of the fable.

filium . . . manere fecit: cf. G. 3.1.

237 *notitiam posset habere:* LL periphrastic verb form (*notitiam habeo =
nosco,* cf G. 2.2.1), "so that he could know."

238 *sibi = ei* (cf. G. 4.1): *sibi* refers to the prince in the cave.

235 *uix (adv.)* with difficulty

peritus, -a, -um (adj.) experienced

medicus, i, m. doctor, physician

infra (prep + acc) below, under

sol, solis, m. sun

luna, ae, f. moon

priuo, -are, -aui, -atum deprive

236 *petra, ae, f.* rock

spelunca, ae, f. cave

excido, -ere, -cidi, -cisum cut out

usque (adv.) continuously

237 *finio, -ire, -iui, -itum* finish

genus, eris, n. kind, sort

adduco, -ere, -duxi, -ductum bring

notitia, ae, f. knowledge

238 *aurum, i, n.* gold

argentum, i, n. silver

lapis, idis, m. stone

pretiosus, -a, -um (adj.) precious

uestis, is, f. garment

unusquisque (pron.) each and every

nomen, inis, n. name

minister, i, m. servant

indico, -are, -aui, -atum tell

*Some time passes. The prince is probably in his teens when he encounters women
for the first time and asks what they are called. The king's sword-bearer tells him
that they are "demons who lead men astray." At the end of the day, when his
father asks him what he liked best of the things he saw, the prince replies that the
"demons who lead men astray" excited him the most.*

The fable is not about naming women but about the nature of desire: "men will always desire women, even if they do not know what to call them."[32] *The fable is a very ancient one. Some see parallels to it in the Mahābhārata and Rāmāyana.*[33] *It is found in the Arabic version of the legend and is preserved in all subsequent renditions of it. Boccacio uses it in his "Decameron" (introduction to the fourth day), although there the boy is told that the women are called "geese."*[34] *Theodas uses this fable to illustrate to Avenir that women can effectively distract the young prince from his interest in the ascetic life because, just as the prince in the cave was drawn to women without knowing what to call them, so will natural instinct draw Josaphat to these women.*

239 Cum autem nomen mulierum discere anxie quaereret, spatharius regis ludendo dixit daemones eas esse quae homines seducunt. **240** Rege igitur interrogante filium quid de omnibus quae uiderat plus amaret: **241** "Quid", inquit, "pater, aliud nisi daemones illos qui seducunt homines? **242** In nullo enim sicut in his sic exarsit anima mea." **243** Non igitur aliter putes te filium tuum superare nisi hoc modo."

239 *Cum . . . discere quaereret:* LL infinitive of the goal, "Because . . . he was aspiring to learn . . ." (cf. G. 3.3.2).
ludendo: **gerund** in the ablative ("by joking," i.e., "in jest").
240 . . . *quid de omnibus . . . plus amaret:* cf. G. 5.1 for *de omnibus* = **partitive genitive** (". . . what he liked more out of all the things that he had seen").
241 *daemones illos* is grammatically masculine, but refers to the women whom the sword-bearer called in jest *daemones qui seducunt homines.*

239 *nomen, inis, n.* name
mulier, eris, f. woman
anxie (adv.) anxiously
spatharius, ii, m. sword-bearer (LL)
ludo, -ere, lusi, lusum joke
daemon, onis, m./f. spirit, evil spirit
seduco, -ere, -duxi, -ductum seduce
240 *plus (comparative of multus)* more
241 *nisi (conj.)* except
242 *sicut = ut*
exardesco, -ere, -arsi, -arsum burn
243 *aliter (adv.)* in another way
supero, -are, -aui, -atum overcome, conquer

---

32. Lopez and McCracken (2014) 155.
33. Almond (1987) 398. Unfortunately, Almond provides no specific reference.
34. Lopez and McCracken (2014) 154.

The king listens to Theodas and decides to try to crush his son's enthusiasm for ascetic piety with the charms of attractive women.

244 Rex igitur omnibus ministris eiectis puellas decoras ei sociauit quae eum semper ad libidinem prouocabant nec habebat alium ad quem respiceret aut cum quo loqueretur uel cum quo uesceretur. **245** Malignus uero spiritus a mago missus in iuuenem irruit et magnum intus caminum ignis accendit. **246** Malignus igitur spiritus intus inflammabat, puellae autem exterius dirum excitabant ardorem.

244 *ad quem respiceret . . . cum quo . . . cum quo*: **relative clauses of characteristic** ("to whom he could look for advice . . ." etc.).
246 *Malignus igitur spiritus:* here *igitur* has a resumptive meaning, indicating simply transition ("and then"). For the LL weakening of the force of *igitur* compared to CL where it introduces inference or deduction, cf. G. 7.8.

244 *eicio, -iere, -ieci, -iectum* throw out, eject
socio, -are, -aui, -atum join, associate
respicio, -ere, -spexi, -spectum consider, look for advice
uescor, uesci eat
245 *malignus, -a, -um (adj.)* wicked
irruo, -ere, -rui invade, rush into
magus, i, m. magician
caminus, i, m. fireplace, fire
accendo, -ere, -cendi, -censum kindle
246 *intus (adv.)* inside
exterius (adv.) on the outside
dirus, -a, -um (adj.) horrible, cruel
excito, -are, -aui, -atum arouse
ardor, oris, m. heat (of passion)

Josaphat resists the temptations with divine help. Theodas now sends to Josaphat an especially attractive orphaned princess, who promises to convert to Christianity if Josaphat agrees to have sex with her. She argues that even the prophets had wives and that the apostle Peter had a wife as well. The sex for conversion motif plays no role in the Buddhist version but appears in the Arabic and all Christian versions of the legend.[35]

---

35. Lopez and McCracken (2014) 153.

247 Qui se tam fortiter uexari sentiens turbabatur et deo se totum recommendans diuinam consolationem recepit et omnis temptatio abscessit. **248** Deinde quandam puellam pulcherrimam cuiusdam regis filiam, sed patre orbatam ad eum misit. **249** Cui cum uir dei <u>praedicaret</u> illa respondit: **250** "Si me ab <u>idolorum</u> cultura saluare desideras, coniungere mihi nuptiarum copulā. **251** Nam et Christiani coniugia non abhorrent, sed laudant, quia <u>patriarchae</u> eorum et <u>prophetae</u> et Petrus eorum apostolus coniuges habuerunt."

247 *Qui:* **connecting relative**, refers to Josaphat.
248 *misit:* the subject is the magician Theodas.
249 *uir dei* ("the man of god"): refers to Josaphat.
250 *coniungere:* passive imperative of *coniungo* "be joined to me. . . ."
251 *Nam et Christiani: et = etiam* (even), cf. G. 7.9.

247 *fortiter (adv.)* strongly
uexo, -are, -aui, -atum shake, harass
turbo, -are, -aui, -atum disturb, throw into confusion
recommendo, -are, -aui, -atum entrust
diuinus, -a, -um (adj.) divine
consolatio, onis, f. comfort
recipio, -ere, -cepi, -ceptum receive
temptatio, onis, f. temptation
abscedo, -ere, -cessi, -cessum depart
248 *orbo, -are, -aui, -atum* deprive of
249 *praedico, -are, -aui, -atum* preach
respondeo, -ere, -di, -sponsum reply
250 *cultura, ae, f.* worship
saluo, -are, -aui, -atum save
desidero, -are, -aui, -atum require
coniungo, -ere, -iunxi, -iunctum unite
nuptiae, arum, f. (pl.) marriage
copula, ae, f. bond, tie
251 *Christianus, -a, -um (adj.)* Christian
coniugium, ii, n. marriage
abhorreo, -ere, -horrui be averse to
patriarcha, ae, m. patriarch
propheta, ae, m. prophet
apostolus, i, m. apostle
coniunx, iugis, m./f. husband or wife

The orphan princess comes close to seducing Josaphat.

252 Ad quam ille: "Inaniter, mulier, ista mihi prosequeris. **253** Permittitur quidem christianis uxores ducere, sed non his qui promiserunt Christo uirginitatem seruare." **254** Et illa: "Sit ita ut uis; **255** sed, si animam meam saluare desideras, unam minimam petitionem mihi perfice, concumbe mecum tantum hac nocte et promitto tibi quod summo diluculo efficiar christiana. **256** Nam si, ut dicitis, gaudium est angelis in caelo super uno peccatore paenitentiam agente, auctori conuersionis nonne magna merces debetur? **257** Semel tantum mihi acquiesce et sic me ipsam saluabis." **258** Illa igitur turrim animae illius fortiter commouere coepit. **259** Quod daemon uidens sociis suis ait: **260** "Videtis quomodo puella ista concussit quae nos non potuimus concutere. **261** Venite ergo et in eum fortiter irruamus ex quo congruum tempus inuenimus."

254 *promitto quod*: cf. G. 3.2.
255 *quod*: What clause is this? (Cf. G. 3.2).
summo diluculo: "at the crack of dawn."
256 *gaudium est angelis in caelo super uno peccatore paenitentiam agente*: cf. Luke 15:7 and 10.
260 *quomodo* + LL **indirect question** without subjunctive (cf. G. 3.4).
quae nos non potuimus concutere: **relative noun clause** as DO of *concussit*.
261 *ex quo*: introduces *LL* causal clause (cf. G. 3.5.3) = CL **causal clause** with *quod, quia, quoniam*.

252 *inaniter (adv.)* in vain, uselessly
prosequor, -sequi, -secutus sum tell
253 *quidem (adv.)* indeed
uxor, oris, f. wife (*uxorem ducere* marry)
promitto, -ere, -misi, -missum promise
uirginitas, tatis, f. virginity
seruo, -are, -aui, -atum keep, reserve
255 *minimus, -a, -um (adj.)* smallest, least (superlative of *parvus, -a, -um*)
petitio, onis, f. request
perficio, -ere, -feci, -fectum accomplish, complete
concumbo, -ere, -cubui, -cubitum have intercourse with
tantum (adv.) only
hac (adv.) this way, in this way
diliculum, i, n. dawn, break of day
256 *poenitentia, ae, f.* penance; (+ *ago*) do penance, repent
auctor, oris, m. originator, author
merces, cedis, f. reward
debeo, -ere, -ui, -itum (here) owe
257 *semel (adv.)* once, on one occasion

acquiesco, -ere, -eui, -etum submit, make peace with
saluo, -are, -aui, -atum save
258 *turris, is, f.* tower (i-stem noun with acc. sg. turrim)
260 *concutio, -ere, -cussi, -cussum* shatter, weaken
261 *irruo, -ere, -rui, -rutum* charge, attack
congruus, -a, -um (adj.) fitting, suitable

Part 9: Josaphat's Divine Dream and King Avenir's Conversion

Tormented by the temptations caused by Theodas's army of demons, Josaphat turns to prayer and, exhausted, falls asleep. In his dream, he has a vision of both heaven and hell.

262 Cernens igitur sanctus iuuenis se tam fortiter captiuatum quia et concupiscentia incitabat et salus unius puellae, diabolo suggerente, ipsum commouebat, lacrimis infusus orationi se dedit. **263** In qua oratione obdormiens uidit se duci in quoddam pratum decoris floribus exornatum ubi folia arborum dulcem sonum reddebant, aurā quadam gratā agitata et odor mirificus emanabat, ubi fructus uisu speciosissimi et gustu desiderabiles, ubi sedes positae erant auro et gemmis fabricatae, lecti lucidi cum pretiosissimis ornamentis, aquae limpidissimae praeterfluentes. **264** Dehinc in ciuitatem ipsum introduxerunt, cuius muri ex auro obrizo erant quod claritate mirabili refulgebat, ubi aetherei quidam exercitus canticum cantantes quod auris mortalium non audiuit, dictumque est: **265** "Iste est locus beatorum." **266** Cum autem uiri uellent eum reducere, rogabat ut ibi eum manere permitterent. **267** Qui dixerunt: **268** "Cum labore multo adhuc uenies huc, si tamen tibi uim inferre poteris." **269** Deinde ad loca taeterrima ipsum duxerunt omni foeditate plena dictumque est: **270** "Iste est locus iniustorum."

262 *concupiscentia incitabat:* supply *eum* (i.e., Josaphat)
263 *aurā quadam gratā agitata:* take the participle with *folia* ("the leaves, moved by some pleasant breeze").
et after *agitata* connects *reddebant* and *emanabat.*
ubi . . . desiderabiles: supply *erant.*
uisu: **supine** with *speciosissimi* ("extremely beautiful to behold").
gustu: **ablative of specification (respect)**, i.e., "desirable in respect to taste."
sedes . . . fabricatae: discontinuous noun-phrase (cf. G. 6.3). The ablatives *auro et gemmis* describe the material from which the seats were made. CL uses the ablative of material without preposition only in poetry (A&G 403.2.1); in prose, it uses the genitive of material (A&G 344).
265 *iste* has lost its CL pejorative connotations (cf. G. 4.2).

268 *adhuc uenies huc*: the use of the two synonymous adverbs is redundant.
si tamen = si modo ("if only").
si tamen tibi uim inferre poteris: "only if you will be able to do violence to your
own self (take control of yourself). . . ." The prince will have to control his
lower desires to arrive to the beautiful paradise that he saw in his dream.
foeditate plena: the adjective *plenus* takes ablative in CL as well ("full of +
abl").
269 *dictum est*: impersonal verb "it was said."

262 *captiuo, -are, -aui, -atum* take captive
salus, salutis, f. safety, salvation
diabolus, i, m. devil (LL from Greek *diabolos*)
suggero, -ere, -gessi, -gestum excite, advise
lacrima, ae, f. tear
infundo, -ere, -fudi, -fusum wet, moisten *(= perfundo)*
oratio, onis, f. prayer
263 *obdormio, -ire, iui* fall asleep
pratum, i, n. meadow
decorus, -a, -um (adj.) beautiful
exorno, -are, -aui, -atum adorn
folium, ii, n. leaf
sonus, i, m. sound
reddo, -ere, -didi, -ditum return
aura, ae, f. breeze
gratus, -a, -um (adj.) pleasant
mirificus, -a, -um (adj.) wonderful
emano, -are, -aui, -atum waft into the air
fructus, us, m. fruit
speciosus, -a, -um (adj.) beautiful
gustus, us, m. taste
desiderabillis, -e (adj.) desirable
sedes, is, f. seat
aurum, i, n. gold
gemma, ae, f. precious stone
lectus, i, m. bed, couch
lucidus, -a, -um (adj.) transparent
pretiosus, -a, -um (adj.) precious
limpidus, -a, -um (adj.) clear
praeterfluo, -ere flow past
264 *obrizus, -a, -um (adj.)* fine

aethereus, -a, -um (adj.) ethereal, heavenly
canticum, i, n. song
exercitus, us, m. (here) swarm, crowd (CL army)
auris, is, f. ear
265 *beatus, -a, -um (adj.)* blessed
266 *reduco, -ere, -duxi, -ductum* drag away
268 *adhuc = huc (adv.)* to this place, here
infero, -ferre, -tuli, -latum impose (*uim infero* lay violent hands upon)
269 *taeter, -tra, -trum (adj.)* foul, ugly
foeditas, tatis, f. foulness, ugliness

When he wakes up from his dream, Josaphat finds the orphan princess and the other women repulsive. Thus he passes the test of virginity. The role of the dream is very different in the Buddhist version. Prince Siddhārtha has five dreams portending his enlightenment on the night when he has sex with his wife and conceives his son. By contrast, the divine dream protects Josaphat from the charms of all women and helps him preserve his chastity.[36]

In some respects, the episodes are similar to each other. To attain enlightenment, the Buddha had to gain an upper hand over Lust, Craving, and Discontent, the three daughters of Māra, god of desire and death.[37] *They retreat in humiliation just as the demons sent by the magus Theodas return to him in defeat, conquered by Josaphat's resolve (cf. Introd. 1.2.1).*

After seeing that Josaphat has conquered all sexual temptations, Theodas converts. The king gives up his efforts to sway Josaphat away from Christianity and gives him half of his kingdom.

271 Cum autem euigilasset, pulchritudo illius <u>puellae</u> et ceterarum stercore <u>foeditior</u> ei uidebatur. **272** Verum cum maligni spiritus ad Theodam redissent et ipse eos exprobraret, dixerunt: **273** "Priusquam signo crucis signaretur, super ipsum irruentes fortiter ipsum conturbauimus; **274** ut autem se signo crucis muniuit, nos persecutus est cum ira." **275** Tunc Theodas cum rege ad eum intrauit sperans quod ei persuadere posset, sed <u>praedictus</u> magus captus est ab eo quem capere uoluit et ab eo conuersus baptisma suscepit et laudabilem uitam duxit. **276** Rex igitur desperans dimisit ei de consilio amicorum medium regni sui. **277** Ille autem licet desertum tota mente desideraret, tamen propter fidei dilatationem ad tempus ipsum regnum suscepit ac in suis ciuitatibus templa et cruces erexit et omnes ad Christum conuertit.

---

36. Lopez and McCracken (2014) 32.
37. Lopez and McCracken (2014) 41.

271 _foeditior_ = _foedior_: an instance of ungrammatical Latin (cf. G. 8).
273 _priusquam_ + subjunctive expresses time with anticipation (CL): "before he could make a sign with the symbol of the cross . . ." (cf. A&G 551b).
ut autem se signo crucis muniuit: The episode where Josaphat fights the demons and defeats them with the symbol of the cross is omitted. This is one of the few inconsistencies due to Jacobus de Voragine's abridgement of the earlier longer Latin versions.
275 _quod . . . posset_: LL **indirect statement** = CL _se ei persuasurum esse_ (cf. G. 3.2). _persuadere posset_: LL pleonastic use of _possum_ + infinitive (cf. G. 2.2.2) with a future nuance similar to the compound futures listed in G. 2.3.
praedictus: Cf. G. 7.1.
276 _de consilio amicorum_: LL use of the preposition _de_. Translate "according to the advice of his friends" (cf. G. 5.1).
277 _licet_ + subjunctive functions as a concessive conjunction here ("although"). This feature is common in CL as well, but the tense of the subjunctive has to be present or perfect (cf. A&G 527b). The imperfect subjunctive here is a LL feature.
ad tempus ipsum: _ad tempus_ is an Augustinian idiom that refers specifically to a thing happening in secular/worldly time. With _ipsum_, the phrase means "temporarily, for the time being."

271 _euigilo, -are, -aui, -atum_ wake up
272 _malignus, -a, -um (adj.)_ spiteful, wicked
exprobro, -are, -aui, -atum reproach
273 _super (prep + acc)_ upon, over
conturbo, -are, -aui, -atum disturb
274 _munio, -ire, -iui, -itum_ fortify, strengthen
275 _intro, -are, -aui, -atum_ go (CL enter)
magus, i, m. magician
baptisma, atis, n. baptism (LL from Greek _baptisma_)
276 _dimitto, -ere, -misi, -missum_ give up
consilium, ii, n. advice
medium, ii, n. (subst. from medius, -a, -um) half
277 _licet (conj. + subjunctive)_ although
dilatatio, onis, f. increase, dissemination
erigo, -ere, -rexi, -rectum build, erect

Part 10: Josaphat Becomes a Saint

The king converts to Christianity and Josaphat retreats to the desert. The devil attacks Josaphat in several ways.

278 Pater autem tandem filii rationibus et praedicationibus assensum praebens, fidem Christi recepit et baptismum suscipiens et totum regnum filio dimittens ipse paenitentiae operibus uacabat et post hoc laudabiliter uitam finiuit. **279** Iosaphat autem Barachiam regem pronuntians pluries fugere uoluit, sed semper a populo captus uix tandem ualuit. **280** Cum igitur per desertum pergeret, cuidam pauperi regalem habitum dedit et ipse in pauperrima ueste remansit. **281** Diabolus autem multas ei parabat insidias; **282** aliquando enim gladio euaginato in eum irruebat et percutere minabatur nisi desisteret, aliquando in forma ferarum apparebat frendens et dirum mugitum emittens. **283** Ille autem dicebat: **284** "Dominus mihi adiutor est. **285** Non timebo quid faciat mihi homo."

278 *rationibus et praedicationibus:* **datives of indirect object** with *praebens*.
279 *Barachiam:* this is the first time we hear about this character in our abridged version, another detail that Jacobus de Voragine overlooked. We know from the long Latin version[38] that Barachias was a devout Christian and was the only person who came to the aid of fake Barlaam (i.e., Nachor) to defend Christianity during the debates with the pagan orators.
regem: **object complement** with **factitive verb** *pronuntians* ("proclaiming Barachias king").
ualuit = supply *fugere* which we borrow from the previous clause due to the presence of parallelism. *Valeo* here = *possum* (cf. G. 3.3.1)
282 *aliquando . . . aliquando:* at one time . . . at another time.
nisi desisteret: "if he did not give up (the fight with the devil)."
284 *Dominus mihi adiutor est:* language from Psalm 117.6.
285 *quid faciat mihi homo:* unusual **indirect question** governed by *timebo* ("I will not fear what man does to me"). CL would have used a **relative noun clause** with *quod* instead of the question word *quid. Quid* in CL can only be interpreted as introducing **indirect question.**

278 *ratio, onis, f.* argument
praedicatio, onis, f. preaching
assensus, us, m. approval, assent
praebeo, -ere, -bui, -bitum present, show

---

38. de la Cruz Palma (2001) 390, chapter 234.

baptismum, i, n.= baptisma baptism (LL from Greek *baptisma*)
paenitentia, ae, f. penance
uaco, -are, -aui, -atum be free to devote oneself to (+ dat)
laudabiliter (adv.) in a praiseworthy fashion
279 *Barachias, ae, m.* Barachias (personal name)
pluries (adv.) often, frequently
uix (adv.) with difficulty
tandem (adv.) finally
ualeo, -ere, ualui = possum, posse, potui (cf. G. 3.3.1)
280 *pergo, -ere, -rexi, -rectum* proceed, go on
281 *diabolus, i, m.* devil (LL from Greek *diabolos*)
insidiae, arum, f. (pl.) treachery, snare
282 *euagino, -are, -aui, -atum* unsheathe
percutio, -ere, -cussi, -cussum strike, pierce
minor, -ari, -atum threaten
desisto, -ere, -stiti, -stitum give up, stop
fera, ae, f. wild beast
frendo, -ere, -dui gnash the teeth
dirus, -a, -um (adj.) fierce
mugitus, us, m. bellowing, roaring
284 *adiutor, oris, m.* assistant, helper

Josaphat and Barlaam meet again.

286 Duobus igitur annis in heremo Iosaphat uagabundus mansit nec Barlaam inuenire potuit, tandem speluncam inuenit et ante ostium stans dicebat: **287** "Benedic, pater, benedic!" **288** Cuius uocem Barlaam audiens foras exiliit et osculantes se feruentissimis sese alterutrum amplexibus constringebant nec satiari poterant. **289** Retulit autem Iosaphat Barlaam omnia q̲u̲a̲e̲ acciderant et ille immensas gratias egit deo.

286 *uagabundus*: **subject complement** (i.e., predicate adjective) with subject *Josaphat* and *mansit* used as a **linking verb**.
287 *benedic*: imperative of *benedico*.
288 *osculantes se* . . . ; *sese constringebant*: take *se* and *sese* with *alterutrum* to mean "each other," "mutually."

286 *heremus, i, m.* wilderness, desert (LL from Greek *erēmos*)
uagabundus, -a, -um (adj.) wandering
tandem (adv.) finally, at last (here as a conj. "until finally")
287 *benedico, -ere, -dixi, -dictum* bless

288 *foras (adv.)* out of doors, out
exilio, -ire, -ivi leap
osculor, -ari, -atus sum kiss
alteruter, -tra, -trum (adj.) one of two
constringo, -ere, -strinxi, -strictum (here) embrace; bind
satio, -are, -aui, -atum satisfy, sate
289 *refero, -ferre, -tuli, -latum* report, relate
gratia, ae, f. thanksgiving (*gratias ago + dat* thank)

The conclusion of the legend of Barlaam and Josaphat. The details that appear here were first added in the Greek version that greatly expanded the narrative of Josaphat's death. Medieval audiences enjoyed reading about miracles that happened at the graves of saints and martyrs, a contributing factor to the legend's enduring popularity (cf. Introd. 3.3).[39]

290 Mansit autem Iosaphat ibidem annis multis in abstinentia mirabili et uirtute, tandem completis diebus Barlaam in pace quieuit circa annos domini CCCLXXX. **291** Iosaphat igitur in anno XXV regnum deserens triginta quinque annis heremiticum laborem subiit et sic multis clarus uirtutibus in pace quieuit et cum corpore Barlaam positus fuit. **292** Quod audiens rex Barachias illuc cum multo exercitu uenit et corpora reuerenter assumens in ciuitatem suam transtulit, ad quorum tumulum miracula multa fiunt.

290 *circa annos domini CCCLXXX*: this date of 380 CE for the death of Barlaam is fictional. It associates Jacobus's version of the legend with 4th-century CE Desert monasticism that flourished in Egypt. The longer versions make no mention of a date. Cf. Introd. 3.2.

290 *ibidem (adv.)* in that very place
abstinentia, ae, f. abstinence
291 *desero, -ere, -serui, -sertum* abandon, leave
heremiticus, -a, -um (adj.) solitary, monastic
subeo, -ire, -i(v)i, -itum undergo
292 *reuerenter (adv.)* reverently
assumo, -ere, -sumpsi, -sumptum take up
transfero, -ferre, -tuli, -latum transport (in the Middle Ages, the practice of
    transporting the remains of a saint was called *translatio*)
tumulus, i, m. tomb

---

39. Lopez and McCracken (2014) 136.

Fig. 3. The heyday of the legend's popularity was over by the end of the 16th century, but this etching shows that Barlaam and Josaphat remained a source of inspiration for artists into the 17th century. Jacques Callot (c.1592–1635), *Saints Barlaam and Josaphat* Etching 7.6 × 4.9 cm (3 × 1 15/16 in.).

Harvard Art Museums/Fogg Museum, Gift of William Gray from the collection of Francis Calley Gray, by exchange, S3.35.8. Photo: Imaging Department © President and Fellows of Harvard College.

Appendix

In the following four examples of long periodic sentences, the nested dependent clauses are articulated in a way that shows the hierarchy of their dependence upon each other. The main clause is flush left. Each dependent clause is indented in a way that puts it further to the right than the clause upon which it depends. The left alignment of words means that all the words aligned with each other belong inside the same dependent clause. This is a useful tracking tool when a clause is interrupted by one or more clauses that depend on it.

Example 1: Chapter 36

The jealous courtiers are addressing the king. They are the subject of *inquiunt*:

"Sed si
    hoc,"
inquiunt,
    "ita esse,   **indirect statement**
   o rex, scire desideras,   end of **simple condition**
ipsum secreto aduoca et
    uitam hanc cito finiendam   **indirect statement**
commemora et idcirco   (this *et* connects *commemora* and *asseras*)
    gloriam regni te uelle derelinquere et monachorum habitum assumere
                               indirect statement
asseras
      quos tamen ignoranter hactenus fueras persecutus
                            relative adjectival clause with
                               monachorum
et tunc uidebis
    quid tibi responderit."   **indirect question**

Example 2: Chapter 38

Quod rex audiens et   *quod* is **connecting relative**, DO of
                                       participial clause
    uerum esse   **indirect statement** with *credens*
        quod illi dixerant   **relative noun clause**, subject of the
                                       indirect statement
credens,   **participial clause**
furore repletus est, nihil tamen sibi respondit.

Example 3: Chapter 86

O stulte,
  si <u>praeconem</u> fratris tui,
    cui
        nihil te deliquisse   **indirect statement**
      cognoscis,   **relative adjectival clause** with *fratris*
    adeo timuisti,   **simple condition**
quomodo <u>praecones</u> domini mei,
    in quem adeo peccaui,   **relative adjectival clause** with *domini*
timere non debeam,
      qui sonabilius mihi tubā mortem significant et terribilem iudicis aduentum
      denuntiant?   **relative adjectival clause** with *praecones*

Example 4: Chapter 114

Qui delectationes corporales desiderant et
  animas suas fame mori permittunt,   **relative noun clause**, subject of *sunt*
similes sunt cuidam homini
  qui,   **relative adjectival clause**
    dum a facie unicornis   **temporal clause**
      ne ab eo deuoraretur   **purpose clause**
    uelocius fugeret,
  in quodam baratrum magnum cecidit.

Grammar

Grammar

Late Latin Features and Favored Classical Constructions

1. Orthography

The orthography of Late and Medieval Latin did not change much from Classical Latin. Note that in the vocabulary and commentary version of the text, all words are adjusted to accord with the Classical Latin norm. Listed below are some of the changes visible in the original version printed at the beginning of the reader:

1.1. The diphthongs *ae* and *oe* are regularly reduced to *e* (e.g., *equitas* = *aequitas*, justice; *cepit* = *coepit*, began).

1.2. *hiis* = *his*. The form arises from confusion with *iis/eis* due to the silent *h*, which even in the classical period was not voiced.[1]

1.3. *i* in some Greek words is replaced by *y* (e.g., *hystoria, ydoli*).[2]

1.4. consonant redoubling (e.g., *connuoco* = *conuoco*, i.e., *convoco*).[3]

1.5. *u* stands for both *u* and *v* (e.g., *uir* = *vir*). The use of *u* for *v* is a standard way of printing classical texts as well. The text of the legend in Maggioni's edition strictly complies with the following rule:

> "Until the seventeenth and eighteenth centuries the letter forms i/j and u/v were not used, as now, to distinguish vowels and consonants: *u* was normal for both the vowel /u/ and the consonant /v/; *v*, if used at all, is in initial place for both /u/ and /v/...."[4]

---

1. Cf. Dinkova-Brunn (2011) 296.
2. Cf. Dinkova-Brunn (2011) 294.
3. Cf. Dinkova-Brunn (2011) 296.
4. Rigg (1996) 79.

Therefore, in our text:

> *v* becomes *u* in the middle of words (e.g., *inuenit* = *invenit*)
> lower case *v* becomes *u* at the beginning of words (e.g., *uir* = *vir*)
> capital *v* remains *v* (e.g., *Vir* = *Vir*).
> capital *u* becomes *v* (e.g., *Vnus* = *Unus*)

2. *Morphology*

2.1. PERFECT PASSIVE TENSES WITH AUXILIARY VERBS *FUIT* AND *FUERAT*

While this is not a LL feature, Late and Medieval Latin often interprets forms like *amata est* as "she is loved" instead of "she was loved" or "she has been loved" (CL), retaining the literal sense of the auxiliary verb *esse* and preserving the adjectival nature of the participle. Therefore LL began to resort more frequently than CL to the substitution of *est* with *fuit* and *erat* with *fuerat* in the passive forms of the perfect tenses:[5]

> E.g.,   captus fuit = *captus est*
>   captus fuerat = *captus erat*
>   captus fuerit = *captus erit*

2.2. PERIPHRASTIC VERB FORMS

The use of "pleonastic auxiliary verbs" is common in LL due to a preference for analytic over synthetic forms.[6] In this text, we find the pleonastic use of *debeo*, *possum*, *habeo*, and *facio*. When translating into English, the original meaning of the pleonastic auxiliary verb can be ignored.

2.2.1. Periphrastic Compounds with a Noun + *habeo*,[7] *ago*,[8] *facio*[9]

> E.g.,   **notitiam habeo** (73, 237) = *nosco*
>   **spem habeo** (225) = *spero*
>   **curam ago** (34) = *curo*

---

5. Cf. Rigg (1996) 85 pt. 3 and Dinkova-Brunn (2011) 300.
6. Cf. Elliott (1997) 40 pt. 7.2.
7. Cf. Elliott (1997) 13–14 pt. 2.4.1.
8. Cf. Elliott (1997) 14 pt. 2.4.3.
9. Cf. Elliott (1997) 114 pt. 2.4.2.

*Rex . . . Arachi amico **notam fecit** filii duritiam* (187)
The king explained (made known) to his friend Arachis the
stubbornness of his son.

2.2.2. Pleonastic Use of *possum* + Infinitive

Our text exhibits the LL leaning toward "periphrasis and preference for analytic
over synthetic forms."[10] The auxiliary status of *possum* may be stronger in some
cases than in others. This is a fluid situation. *Possum* can be viewed as redundant
in the following sentence where instead of *consequi posses* CL would have used
consequereris:

> E.g., . . . *quae si diligentius conseruares, magnam inde utilitatem **consequi**
> **posses*** (99)
> If you were to keep these mandates diligently, you would/could
> receive great help from them.

The interpretation of *possum* as auxiliary verb is clearer in the following
example where instead of *possit afferre* CL would have used *afferat* and instead
of *cogitare posset* CL would have used *cogitaret*:

> E.g., . . . *praecipiens illis ut nec mortem nec senectutem nec infirmitatem
> uel paupertatem nec aliquid quod **possit afferre** tristitiam sibi ei
> nominarent, sed omnia iucunda ei proponerent, quatenus mens eius
> laetitiis occupata nihil de futuris **cogitare posset*** (26)
> . . . ordering them to mention to him neither death, nor old age,
> nor illness, nor poverty, nor anything that **would/could cause**
> sadness to him, but to offer him all pleasant things, so that his
> mind, preoccupied with joyful things, **would not think** at all about
> future affairs.

2.2.3. Pleonastic Use of *debeo* + Infinitive

> E.g., *hominem . . . inuenit a quo rogatur ut se **suscipere debeat*** (29)
> He found a man who asked him (the knight) to offer him hospitality.

Suscipere debeat = *suscipiat*. Since *debeat* is redundant, it should be ignored in
translation.

---

10. Cf. Elliott (1997) 40 pt. 7.2.

2.3. COMPOUND FUTURE WITH *DEBEO* AND *VOLO*

These usages are precursors to the compound futures in the Romance languages.[11]

2.3.1. Compound Future with *debeo* + Infinitive[12]

E.g., *Noti sunt igitur qui hoc **pati debeant** an sic indefinite proueniunt?* (56)
Are therefore those who will endure this known or these things happen thus randomly?

2.3.2. Compound Future with *volo* in the Subjunctive + Infinitive[13]

E.g., . . . *si me **dimittere uelles**, tria tibi mandata darem* (99)
If you would let me go, I would give you three mandates.

2.4. FREQUENT USES OF THE FIRST PERIPHRASTIC CONJUGATION (A&G 195) IN LATE LATIN

The First Periphrastic conjugation (A&G 195) with the future active participle becomes more common in LL than the simple future and often replaces it. This process is completed in the formation of the compound futures in the Romance languages.[14]

E.g., *Nam illius quam persequeris <u>christianae</u> religionis, ut <u>aestimo</u>, **futurus est** cultor* (23)
For he will be a worshipper, as I think, of that Christian religion which you persecute.

2.5. GERUNDIVES

In LL, **Gerundives** often lose the connotation of necessity, associated with them in CL.[15]

E.g., *Assideant autem ad audentiam dicendorum prudentia et <u>aequitas</u>* (10)
Let self-control and justice preside over the hearing of the things about to be said.

---

11. Elliott (1997) 41.
12. Cf. Elliott (1997) 41 pt. 7.2.1. (4) and Stotz (1998) vol. 4.325 §61.7.
13. Cf. Elliott (1997) 41 pt. 7.2.1. (3) and Stotz (1998) vol. 4.324 §61.6.
14. Cf. Elliott (1997) 41.
15. Stotz (1998) vol. 4.324 §61.4.

In some cases, the **gerundive** stands simply for the **future active participle**.[16] In our text, there is one example involving the gerundive of obligation, also known as **passive periphrastic** or Second Periphrastic Conjugation (A&G 196) infinitive *finiendam (esse)* = *finituram (esse)*.

> E.g., uitam hanc cito finiendam commemorā (36)
> Remember that this life will soon end.

3. Syntax

3.1. INFINITIVE FOR RESULT CLAUSE WITH *FACIO* = CL **OBJECTIVE INFINITIVE** WITH *IUBEO, COGO, ETC.*[17]

Facio, when it governs LL infinitive for result clause, means "make, order, cause, force, prompt, etc." Its meaning is regularly completed with a passive infinitive, as in English "I had this done." The active infinitive is used in the case of intransitive verbs only. The infinitive for result clause with active infinitive is similar to English: "I will make you come," i.e., "I will force you to come."

> E.g., *Palatium speciosissmum construi fecit* (25)
> He ordered a very luxurious palace to be built OR He had a very luxurious palace be built.
> [*palatium* is the accusative subject of passive infinitive *construi*]
> . . . *prauitas tuae uoluntatis et contentio effrenata aduersus caput meum te insanire fecit* (181)
> The corruption of your will and your unrestrained strife against my person caused you to become insane, i.e., forced you to go out of your mind.
> [*te* is the accusative subject of the active infinitive of intransitive verb *insanire*]

3.2. INDIRECT STATEMENTS WITH *QUOD, QUIA, QUONIAM,* AND *UT* = CL **INDIRECT STATEMENT** WITH ACCUSATIVE + INFINITIVE

While in CL the only way to express **indirect statement** was through the accusative and infinitive construction, LL uses both the CL **indirect statement** and indirect statements with *quod, quia, quoniam,* and *ut*. The mood may be indicative or subjunctive, but generally "*quod* tends to take the subjunctive, *quia* the indicative."[18]

---

16. Stotz (1998) vol. 4.324 §61.5.
17. Elliott (1997) 47 pt. 7.9.3.
18. Elliott (1997) 48 pt. 7.10.1.

E.g.,   . . . *ipsum apud regem accusauerunt* **quod** *non solum ad christianorum*
         fidem declinasset, sed insuper regnum sibi conabatur subripere (35)
     They accused him before the king that not only had he turned
          towards the faith of the Christians, but in addition, that he was
          trying to grab the kingdom for himself.

   Notum tibi sit **quod** *rex suspicatur* **ut** *propter hoc dixeris quod eius*
      regnum uelis inuadere (40)
   Let it be known to you that the king suspects that you said this for
       this reason, because you want to usurp his kingdom.
   Cur, rex, tristaris **quia** *bonorum particeps sum effectus?* (184)
   Why are you sad, king, that I have become a recipient of benefits?

3.3. EXPANDED USE OF THE INFINITIVE

Many of the expanded uses of the infinitive are influenced by infinitive uses in
Greek.

3.3.1. Complementary Infinitive with Verbs That Rarely Take It in CL

   valeo = CL *possum* be able to
   consuesco = CL *soleo* be accustomed to
   molior = CL *conor* try
   scio = CL *possum* be able to
   praesumo = CL *audeo* dare

   E.g.,   . . . *nihil omnino respondere sciuerunt* (220)
        They were able to respond nothing at all.

3.3.2. Infinitive of the Goal[19]

Infinitive of the goal occurs in this text with verbs of seeking, asking, and
fearing. It is influenced by Greek:

   E.g.,   . . . *regem super hoc arguere formidantes* . . . (81)
        fearing to reproach the king about this . . .

   Cum . . . *discere quaereret* (239)
   Because he was aspiring to learn . . .

---

19. Cf. Elliott (1997) p. 47 pt. 7.9.2. Cf. also Rigg (1996) 85 pt. 4 who classifies it as Purpose
Infinitive.

3.4. INDIRECT QUESTION + INDICATIVE = CL **INDIRECT QUESTION** + SUBJUNCTIVE[20]

While this text consistently complies with the CL requirement for subjunctive in **indirect questions**, as in most LL texts, the CL rules governing the subjunctive are not always observed.

> E.g., ... *cum simulato Barlaam ordinassent quomodo prius debebat simulare se fidem christianorum defendere* ... (200)
> ... when they had prescribed for fake Barlaam how he would pretend at first that he was defending the faith of the Christians ...

3.5. SUBORDINATING CONJUNCTIONS

3.5.1. ac si = *tamquam* "as if"[21] Occurs Frequently in LL

> E.g., ... *gratiam tamen agis deo <u>ac si</u> magna recepisses ab eo* (149)
> nevertheless you thank god as if you had received great things from him.

3.5.2. **dum** + Subjunctive = CL **cum/dum** + Indicative

3.5.2.1. In LL, "the use of the subjunctive was sometimes extended to *dum* clauses, even when *dum* means 'while.'"[22] Also, in LL, "*dum* often replaces *cum* and tends to take the subjunctive automatically."[23]

When encountering *dum* + subjunctive, the reader should **not** interpret it according to CL rules, i.e., as time + anticipation ("until") or proviso clause ("provided that"), but as CL *dum*- or *cum*- clause with indicative ("while," "when").

> E.g., *Qui delectationes corporales desiderant et animas suas fame mori permittunt, similes sunt cuidam homini qui, **dum (1)** a facie unicornis ne ab eo deuoraretur uelocius fugeret, in quodam baratrum magnum cecidit. 115 **Dum (2)** autem caderet, manibus arbustulam quandam apprehendit.*

---

20. Cf. Elliott (1997) 49 pt.7.11. See also Godfrey (2003) xiii.
21. Cf. Elliott (1997) 36 pt. 6.1.
22. Cf. Rigg (1996) 85.
23. Harrison (1991) xxvi (v).

We find both possibilities for the interpretation of LL *dum* + subjunctive in these two uses of *dum*:

1. The first *dum* + subjunctive = CL *dum*/*cum* + indicative, "when/while . . . he was running fast"
2. The second *dum* + subjunctive = CL *dum* + indicative, "while he was falling."

3.5.2.2. In addition, LL uses *dum* + *subjunctive* to express cause ("since")[24] = CL *cum* + subjunctive

E.g., *Interea, dum rex liberos non haberet, puer ei pulcherrimus nascitur et Iosaphat appellatur* (19)
In the meantime, since the king had no children, a very handsome boy was born to him and was called Josaphat.

3.5.3. ex quo = CL causal clause with *quod, quia, quoniam*

E.g., *Ex quo tuam uideo pertinaciam nec mihi obedire uis, saltem ueni et ambo pariter ueritati credamus* (196)
Because I see your stubbornness and because you do not wish to obey me, at least come and let us put our trust in truth together.

3.5.4. quod + indicative or Subjunctive[25] Expressing Result = CL *ut* + Subjunctive Expressing result clause

E.g., *Coepit igitur Nachor fidem christianorum euidenter defendere et rationibus communire, ita **quod** rhetores illi muti effecti nihil omnino respondere sciuerunt* (220)
Nachor began to openly defend the faith of the Christians and to support it with arguments in such a way that those orators, having become silent, were able to respond nothing at all.

3.5.5. quod + indicative = CL *ut* + Subjunctive Expressing noun result Clause

E.g., *Erat autem regi consuetudo **quod**, quando aliquis morti tradendus erat, rex ante eius ianuam praeconem cum tuba ad hoc deputata mittebat* (82)

---

24. Sidwell (1995) 372 G. 30(a).
25. For an example of this *quod* with Subjunctive, cf. Elliott (1997) 38.

The king had a custom that when someone was about to be
sentenced to death, he dispatched in front of that person's door a
herald with a trumpet designated for this.

3.5.6. quando = CL *cum* temporal[26]

E.g., See example above from chapter 82.

3.5.7. quatenus = CL *ut* Introducing purpose clause

E.g., ... *praecipiens illis ut nec mortem nec senectutem nec infirmitatem
uel paupertatem nec aliquid quod possit afferre tristitiam sibi ei
nominarent, sed omnia iucunda ei proponerent,* **quatenus** *mens eius
laetitiis occupata nihil de futuris cogitare posset* (26)
... ordering them to mention to him neither death, nor old age, nor
illness, nor poverty, nor anything that would/could cause sadness
to him, but to offer him all pleasant things, **so that** his mind,
preoccupied with joyful things, would not think at all about future
affairs.

3.6. SUBSTANTIVE PARTICIPIAL CLAUSES (PHRASES)

While substantive participles are very common in CL as well, in LL they often
form their own clause with direct objects and/or other elements:

E.g., *Sic ergo stulti sunt illi qui confidunt in idolis quia* **plasmatos a se**
adorant et **custoditos a se** *custodes suos appellant* (112)
In the same way those who trust in idols are foolish because they
worship **those made by them** and they call **those guarded by
them** their guardians.

4. Pronouns

4.1. CARELESS USE OF REFLEXIVE PRONOUN *SE* AND PRONOMINAL ADJECTIVE *SUUS*

"Medieval Latin usage of the reflexives *se* and *suus* is often careless by classical
standards."[27] Sometimes *se* and *suus* conform to CL rules, but often they do
not refer to the subject or agent of their clause as in CL. In LL, "confusion of

26. Cf. Elliott (1997) 38 pt.6.1.
27. Rigg (1996) 86 pt. 7.

reflexive and non-reflexive forms is common, and it was the reflexive forms
which, in general, carried the day in the Romance languages, e.g., *son livre*
(French)."[28] Thus, *se* is often the equivalent of a demonstrative pronoun like *is,
ea, id.*

E.g., *Rex . . . nihil **sibi** respondit* (38)
       The king did not respond anything to him.
       (CL would require the translation "The king did not respond
          anything to himself," an absurd interpretation)

4.2. DEMONSTRATIVES (*IS, HIC, ILLE, ISTE, IPSE*) USED WITHOUT THE CL DISTINCTIONS[29]

These pronouns begin to be used interchangeably. As the following example
shows, *iste* does not always carry the negative connotations it had in CL:

E.g., ***Iste** est locus beatorum* (265)
       This is the place of the blessed ones.
       ***Iste** est locus iniustorum* (279)
       This is the place of the unjust ones.

Ipse can be used indiscriminately for *hic, ille,* or *iste*:

E.g., *. . . salus unius <u>puellae</u>. . . **ipsum** commouebat* (262)
       The salvation of one girl . . . was moving him.

4.3. *IPSE* AS THE DEFINITE ARTICLE[30]

E.g., ***ipsam uirtutem** quam habet uisibilem perdit* (74)
       He loses **the seeing capacity** that he has.

4.4. INDECLINABLE PRONOUN *HUIUSMODI* (THIS THING, SUCH THINGS)

E.g., *. . . plurimum desiderans <u>in huiusmodi</u> dirigi et doceri* (67)
       . . . desiring very much to be directed and taught in this thing/in such
          things.

28. Elliott (1997) 34 pt. 5.3.1.
29. Sidwell (1995) 365 G. 11(c).
30. Sidwell (1995) 365 G. 11(a). *Ille* also can function as the definite article in Medieval Latin, cf. Dinkova-Brunn (2011) 300–301.

5. *Prepositions*

5.1. PREPOSITIONS WITH UNUSUAL MEANINGS

The use of prepositions in LL is unpredictable, but some peculiarities occur with regularity. One should first try to interpret the preposition according to CL rules. *De*, for example, retains the CL meaning of "from" or "about" most of the time. The following peculiarities, however, should be kept in mind:

> **de** + abl with *impleo* "to fill with" = CL ablative or genitive with verbs of
> filling (A&G 409a)
> E.g.,   *Neque enim uentrem tuum <u>de me</u> implere ualebis* (99)
> And you will not be able to fill your stomach with me.

> **de** + abl may also mean "according to"[31]
> E.g.,   *de consilio amicorum* (276)
> according to the advice of his friends

> **e/ex** or **de** + abl = **partitive genitive**[32]

With numerals, CL "often uses e/ex or *de* plus the ablative instead of a **partitive genitive**,"[33] and this scenario is frequent in our text. It is as frequent as the **partitive genitive** is:

> E.g.,   *unus sapientior ex ipsis dixit* (21)
> a wiser one of them said . . .

> **in** + abl = CL **ablative of means** without preposition[34]
> E.g.,   *Si enim aliquis <u>in uerbis</u> laedatur . . .* (33)
> Should someone be hurt with words . . .

> **in** + abl = CL **ablative of time** without preposition
> E.g.,   *in octoginta uel centum annis* (66)
> within eighty or hundred years

> **pro** + abl = CL **ablative of cause** without preposition
> E.g.,   *pro eo* (49) = *propterea*;

---

31. Cf. Stotz (1998) vol. 4.281§ 34 and Adams (2011) 276–70 on the use of de + ablative instead of genitive and also on the instrumental uses of de + ablative.

32. Godfrey (2003) xi, section b-vi-e.

33. Shelmerdine (2013) 103. Cf. Stotz (1998) vol. 4.286 §36.

34. Godfrey (2003) xi, section b-vi-c.

pro inconsuetudine (58)
because of the strangeness.

5.2. COMPOUND PREPOSITIONS[35] AND COMPOUND ADVERBS[36]

de/ a + foris (94) externally, on the outside
de/ab + intus (94) within
e contra (191) to the contrary
insimul (200) together

E.g.,   *uos autem solum quae de foris sunt attenditis et quae deintus sunt non*
        consideratis (94)
        You however pay attention only to things that are outside and do not
        consider the things which are within.

6. Word Order

6.1. TYPES OF EMBEDDING OF DEPENDENT CLAUSES THAT ARE RARE IN CL

A relative clause may be inserted between a genitive noun or pronoun and its
noun, a pattern more common in poetry than prose in CL:

E.g.,   *Nam **illius** quam persequeris **christianae religionis**, ut aestimo,*
        futurus est cultor (23)
        For, as I think, he will be a worshipper of that Christian religion,
        which you persecute.

Clauses may often be embedded even in an **ablative absolute**, something that
rarely happens in CL.

E.g.,   *Rege autem qui essent huius inimici quaerente . . .* (8)
        When the king was asking who his enemies were . . .

6.2. VERB-SUBJECT WORD ORDER

While the postponed subject is common in CL as well, it occurs with noticeable
frequency in this text.

---

35. Cf. Elliott (1997) 29 pt. 4.1.8.
36. Cf. Elliott (1997) 31 pt. 4.2.2.

E.g.,   *Assideant autem ad audentiam dicendorum **prudentia et aequitas*** (10)

Let **self-control and justice** preside over the hearing of the things about to be said.

6.3. FREQUENT OCCURRENCE OF DISCONTINUOUS NOUN PHRASES

"The discontinuous noun phrase is a noun phrase whose components are not adjacent, but are separated by various elements."[37] While this word order pattern is very common in CL, we call attention to it because it is often a stumbling block for Latin readers on the intermediate level. This text contains a great number of this word order pattern:

E.g.,   ***plura** ad hoc **exempla*** (113) many examples to this (effect)

7. Vocabulary

7.1. WORDS FOR DEFINITE ARTICLE "THE"

The following words should not be translated literally, but the definite article "the" should be used in their place:

praefatus aforementioned, "the"
praedictus aforementioned, "the"

7.2. UNUS AS INDEFINITE ARTICLE[38]

E.g.,   . . . *unus leprosus et unus caecus sibi obuiauerunt* (51)
. . . a leper and a blind man came towards him.

7.3. ALTERNATE FORMS OF SUM, ESSE

7.3.1. *existens* as Present Active Participle of *esse*

Since the text is a translation from the Greek and Latin does not have a present active participle of *esse*, the translator uses the participle *existo* for the active participle of the verb *sum*.

---

37. Spevak (2014) 360.
38. Cf. Elliott (1997) 36 pt. 5.6.2 and Dinkova-Brunn (2011) 301.

E.g.,   *via ... tecum **existenti** facilis mihi erit* (44)
        to me, being with you, the road will be easy

7.3.2. *positus* as the Equivalent of the Nonexistent Perfect Passive Participle/Perfect Passive Infinitive of *esse*

E.g.,   ... *dicens se in multa <u>maestitia</u> positum (esse)* (49)
        ... saying that he was in great sadness
        ... *in magno itaque periculo positus* (126)
        ... being in great danger.
        ... *in dolore nimio positus est* (169)
        ... he was in great pain

7.4. QUANTOCIUS (LL ADVERB) AS QUICKLY AS POSSIBLE (FROM QUANTO+OCIUS)

E.g.,   *Nuntians igitur hoc filio regis ipsum ad eum quantocius introduxit* (77)
        Therefore, announcing this to the son of the king, he led him
        (Barlaam) to him (Josaphat).

7.5. LL EXPRESSIONS FOR "IT HAPPENS"

contingit
provenit
occurrit

7.6. LL VERBS OF ORDERING

facio
praecipio
mando

7.7. LL **LINKING VERBS** (VERBS REQUIRING SUBJECT AND PREDICATE)

apparet = *uidetur* (seem)
efficior = *fio* (become)

E.g.,   *Quis unquam pater in filii sui prosperitate tristis apparuit?* (185)
        What father ever seemed sad in the case of his son's success?

        ... *rhetores illi muti effecti nihil omnino respondere sciuerunt* (220)

... those orators, having become silent, were not able to respond in any way at all.

7.8. SHIFT IN THE MEANING OF *IGITUR*

A whole series of functional elements, including the sentence-connector *igitur*, exhibit a shift in meaning in LL.[39] The excessive use of *igitur* in this text in itself constitutes a LL feature. While in CL *igitur* is always the second word in the sentence, in this text it appears in a sentence-initial position as well (e.g., chapters 68, 146). The reader should not assume that *igitur* always introduces an inference or deduction, as it does in CL. While this is most often the case, sometimes it means simply "and then" or signifies transition.[40]

> E.g., *Incipiens **igitur** Barlaam cepit ei de mundi creatione ... multa ponere ... (96)*
> And then, Barlaam, making a start, began to tell him many things about the creation of the world ...

7.9. *ET = ETIAM*

In CL, this feature occurs more in poetry than in prose, while in LL texts it is common in prose as well. There are several instances of it in this text:

> E.g., *Nam et Christiani coniugia non abhorrent ... (251)*
> For even Christians do not shun marriages ...

7.10. *INDE* MAY MEAN "THEREOF," "OF IT/THEM"[41]

> E.g., *magnam inde utilitatem consequi posses (99)*
> you could receive great help from them

8. *Ungrammatical Latin*[42]

Even though the Latinity of this text is of excellent quality, as in most LL texts, there are instances of ungrammatical Latin where the structure and coherence of the sentence violates the grammatical rules of the language.

---

39. Cf. Elliott (1997) 11 pt. 2.2.
40. Cf. Sidwell (1995) 367 G. 14.
41. Godfrey (2003) xi.
42. Cf. Rigg (1996) 89.

The first example has to do with punctuation that is an editorial decision and not truly a flaw of Jacobus de Voragine's Latinity:

E.g.,   *Neque enim uentrem tuum de me implere ualebis, sed, si me dimittere uelles, tria tibi mandata darem, **quae** si diligentius conseruares, magnam inde utilitatem consequi posses* (99)

quae cannot have a syntactic function in the *consequi posses* clause, because the clause already has a subject (*tu*) and DO (*utilitatem*). Only **connecting** (resumptive) **relative** pronouns can have a syntactic function in a dependent clause that immediately follows (i.e., the *si*-clause). Therefore, *quae* does not form a clause of its own but functions as a **connecting** (resumptive) **relative** pronoun. Since connecting relatives must appear at the beginning of a sentence, this ungrammatical sentence can be easily corrected by substituting the comma printed in Maggioni (2007) with a semicolon:

E.g.,   *Neque enim uentrem tuum de me implere ualebis, sed, si me dimittere uelles, tria tibi mandata darem; quae si diligentius conseruares, magnam inde utilitatem consequi posses* (99)

The second example involves simply adding a preposition:

E.g.,   *Assumpto igitur [a] praedicto principe magno exercitu ad quaerendum Barlaam iuit et heremitam illum capiens se Barlaam cepisse dixit* (173)

In this instance, the Ablative Absolute *Assumpto igitur praedicto principe magno exercitu* can only make sense if we add *a* before *praedicto principe* to form an **ablative of agent** inside the **ablative absolute**.

High-Frequency Word List

This list contains words that appear three or more times in the vocabulary.

abscedo, -ere, -cessi, -cessum   depart, leave
adoro, -are, -aui, -atum   worship, adore
aperio, -ire, aperui, apertum   open
assumo, -ere, -sumpsi, -sumptum   receive
aurum, i, n.   gold
ciuitas, tatis, f.   city, town, castle (LL); state, tribe (CL)
desidero, -are, -aui, -atum   desire, want, wish for, require
diuitiae, arum, f. (pl.)   riches, wealth
efficio, -ere, -feci, -fectum   make, bring to pass (passive *efficior = fio* become, cf. G. 7.7)
existimo, -are, -aui, -atum   think, consider, estimate, judge
fames, is, f.   hunger, famine
habitus, us, m.   attire, clothing
heremiticus, -a, -um (adj.)   solitary, monastic (LL)
heremus, i, m.   wilderness, desert (LL from Greek *erēmos*)
idolum, i, n.   idol, image of pagan deity (LL from Greek *eidolon*)
ignoro, -are, -aui, -atum   not to know, be ignorant
induo, -ere, -dui, -dutum   put on (when clothing is the DO)
inuenio, -ire, -ueni, -uentum   find
medicus, i, m.   doctor, physician
mulier, eris, f.   woman
nosco, -ere, noui, notum   know
osculor, -ari, -atus sum   kiss, embrace
palatium, ii, n.   palace
perdo, -ere, -didi, -ditum   lose, destroy, ruin, debilitate
pergo, -ere, -rexi, -rectum   proceed, pursue
periculum, i, n.   danger, trial, test
plurimum (adv.)   much, very much, most of all

praebeo, -ere, -bui, -bitum   offer, grant

praecipio, -ere, -cepi, -ceptum   order

praedico, -are, -aui, -atum   predict, foretell, preach (LL); make known, announce, proclaim (CL)

pretiosus, -a, -um (adj.)   expensive, costly, precious, valuable, expensive

quomodo (question word)   how? why?

ratio, onis, f.   argument, reason

salus, salutis, f.   safety, salvation

seduco, -ere, -duxi, -ductum   lead astray, seduce

supero, -are, -aui, -atum   overcome, defeat

surgo, -ere, -rexi, -rectum   rise; rule, rise to power

suscipio, -ere, -cepi, -ceptum   receive, take home, offer hospitality to (+ DO)

tristis, -e (adj.)   sad

ualeo, -ere, ualui = possum, posse, potui   (cf. G. 3.3.1)

Personal Names and Anonymous Characters

Personal Names

Arachis (170): a friend and advisor to King Auenir. He devises the scheme that calls for fake Barlaam (Nachor) to voluntarily admit defeat in a theological debate and in this way, discredit Christianity in the eyes of Josaphat.

Auenir (passim): the king of the fictional land called "India," idol-worshipper and enemy of Christianity, father of Josaphat.

Barachias (279, 292): the person to whom Josaphat leaves the governance of his kingdom when he retreats into the desert.

Barlaam (passim): a Christian hermit who becomes mentor and teacher to Josaphat. He gains access to the prince in his isolated palace disguised as a merchant selling a magic stone. He tells the six parables to Josaphat.

Josaphat (passim): prince and son of King Auenir and the main protagonist of the legend.

Nachor (201, 205, 220, etc.): pagan hermit and astrologer who looks like Barlaam and plays the role of fake Barlaam upon the request of Arachis. The longer Latin version tells us that Nachor is the teacher of Arachis.

Theodas (230, 275): magus, magician in King Auenir's court, who uses the fable about the blind prince in the cave in order to convince King Auenir to tempt Josaphat with attractive women. He devises the scheme of diverting Josaphat from the pursuit of the monastic way of life by exposing the prince to sexual temptations and by marshalling an army of demons to torment Josaphat with the fire of passions.

Anonymous Characters in the Main Story (Excluding the Parables)

ch. 2–18 **a nobleman and friend of King Auenir** who becomes a Christian monk.

ch. 19–27 an **astrologer** who correctly predicts the future of Josaphat.

ch 28–47 **a knight (miles)** at Avenir's court who is secretly Christian and a victim of the intrigues of a group of jealous courtiers.

ch 28–47 **a word-mender** or "doctor of words" who helps the Christian knight save face before the king and neutralize the malicious intrigues of the envious courtiers.

ch. 67–76 **Josaphat's tutor** (*paedadagogus*) who gives Barlaam access to Josaphat.

ch. 249–261 **beautiful orphan princess** who nearly succeeds in winning Josaphat over and enticing him to have sex with her.

47331757R00099

Made in the USA
Middletown, DE
06 June 2019